POW 253

ONE MAN'S QUEST FOR LIFE DURING WORLD WAR II

Dare K. Kibble

October 7, 1921 — November 2, 2003

Completed December 22, 1995

Produced by Maggie Kibble Newhouse

POW 253: One Man's Quest for Life during World War II
By Dare K. Kibble
© 2016 by Margaret Lea (Kibble) Newhouse

Print ISBN: 978-0-9970078-0-0
eBook ISBN: 978-0-9970078-1-7

Lead Editor: Jennifer Regner
Cover and Interior Design by: Fusion Creative Works, fusioncw.com

Produced by Maggie Kibble Newhouse

First Printing
Printed in the United States of America

To my family and those who served this great country with me

CONTENTS

Yet you do not know what your life will be like tomorrow...
You are just a vapor which appears for a little
while and then vanishes away.

James 4:14

WHY MY FATHER WROTE THIS BOOK

By Maggie Kibble Newhouse

My dad wanted people to know that, at the time of the war, he was just everybody's kid—he was the next door neighbor, he was the kid who delivered your newspaper, he was the kid your kids played with, he was the student you taught, the kid in the ROTC program, the kid who took your daughter to the prom. He wasn't very old when he went off to war; he was nineteen. Writing this book helped him release a lot of demons. In 1945, PTSD wasn't really known at the time. People just came back and went on with their lives, and they buried those demons. My dad was a voice for many who didn't write down their stories. He did like to write, so it was an outlet for him, but it helped him to exorcise some of those demons. It took him his whole life to do; he completed it in 1995, and passed away in 2003.

His message really is that freedom isn't free; people paid with their lives for it. Some of them didn't lose their lives over it, but they still paid for it. Someone defends that freedom for us every day. Today, we have the rights and privileges we have because soldiers from every war paid for it. You have those rights, because someone like my dad did that for four years—he gave his life for that. We need to remember that, when we think it's alright to burn the flag, or dishonor the flag, or dishonor your country. If you don't want to stand behind your troops, be prepared to stand in front of them.

My dad always believed in the military, regardless of some of the things he writes. I do honestly believe that he felt that what he did was the right thing to do, that he made the best decision at the time. He believed in his country, and why we need a military. He believed in the constitution. He encouraged his sons to join the military, and they both did; my brother retired from the Army, and my other brother served in the Navy. One brother is buried in Arlington National Cemetery. My daughter served in the Army and is a decorated veteran, and I have a son who is currently serving embassy duty in the Marines. My dad felt that being in the military was a good thing; it taught you a lot about yourself. It will *make* you—it will show you what you really want, or what you don't want.

Coming from an educated man, the content of this book is very graphic. My dad wanted people to know what war is like. He wanted to make sure that kids today, who read his book, know that this was all done for killing. Guns are meant to kill. War kills people. It's not a game.

(From Dare Keane Kibble's daughter, Maggie Kibble Newhouse)

THE WORLD WITHIN

You observe one day a life deviate

A World never seen by your soul

Of peace, love, grace and Protector

A "World Within" as a goal.

— dkk

INTRODUCTION

. . . Then all hell broke loose! The ass on the guy in front of me disappeared. It was completely blown away. I could hear and see the slugs hitting all around me along with fragmentation bombs. Then the guy behind me yelled and fell. I was scared shitless and knew I would be next. The planes on the strip were exploding and burning as I ran past them. I looked up at the bombers and knew I could see the gunners sighting in on me. If only those damn machine-gun slugs would stop whining and thudding. How in the hell did I ever get into this mess? Here I was on a spit of an island, in a war I knew nothing about, with death burning down my neck. My only thought was to run, run, run . . . .

CHAPTER 1

Livin' on Steel

As in the life of most young men and women, one of the landmark occasions is the leaving of high school. I had very few friends in high school and looked forward to entering a fresh, electrifying world of choices, i.e., sins, beauty, judgments, morals, corruption, truths, passions, learning and love. Most of the faces of high school days would never be seen again, except on the fabric of the mind in those flashbacks of memory of gone-by days, triggered by a myriad of tidbits in life. I wonder why the Creator placed this feature in our complex composition, I wonder why?

On the night of my graduation in 1940 from Boise High School, I had on my other pair of shoes and new suit. My mother had managed to buy me a new suit and a pair of shoes for graduation. I never did know where she acquired the money for them. I was to ride to graduation with two of my friends. I had been secretly in love with the girl, forever, it seemed. My friend had a 1940 Ford Tudor sedan, black and trimmed in red. Boy, was it a beautiful machine, V8 motor and synchromesh transmission.

Anyway, we were driving down East Jefferson while my friends were chomping their gums at each other and the driver was not paying attention to his driving. A car hit us at an intersection, in the left-hand rear fender, thereby rolling us down Jefferson Street for about 100 feet. It demolished the Ford. My friend's mother was riding in back with me and her head was wedged between the top of the back seat and the flattened roof.

When I felt the car rolling, I grabbed the floor footrest and held on. I was not hurt, except for my new suit (which had a rip in the leg). I was able to get the mother's head free and help her out of the car. My friends were still arguing about the wreck. Can you believe they were later married? I heard later their marriage was pretty rocky, like the Grand Canyon.

Some passerby took us to the graduation ceremony, which was just about over by the time we arrived there. I did get my diploma, however.

After the graduation ceremony, I went outside on the front sidewalk and talked to my father. At the time he told me there was no way he could send me to college. He said the United States was going to war soon and if he were me, he would pick the service where I wanted to fight during the coming conflict.

I was already a member of the Idaho 148th Field Artillery, National Guard, and had been since 1939. We had been told the Guard would be nationalized in September 1940. The only way to receive a discharge from the Guard was to join one of the regular services.

I remember, in the Guard every so often, we would be paid (I think we accrued about three dollars a drill day). On payday a bunch of us would hop the local switching freight train (between Nampa and Boise) and invade the cathouses; a-a-a-a-ah for youth.

On one dark, spring night at about one in the morning, we tried to catch the turnaround freight and the darn train was gaining speed so fast when it went by me, I missed the ladder and spent the night sleeping out. I "hitched" a ride the next morning and was home before my mother was out of bed.

Anyway, after my talk with my father on the night of graduation, I decided to join the Navy. The man who lived next door to my folks had been in the Navy during the early 1930s at sea on board the battleship *Idaho*. He told me, at least in the Navy, I would always have a good, clean bed and meals and, provided I learned to swim, would have a half a chance to come out of the stinking war alive. This was to be the biggest misstatement of fact in the coming years which ever came out of a person's mouth.

On June 27, 1940, my mother (Meatball, we called her, but there was never a mother who was loved any more in this world than she was), put me on a train heading for Salt Lake City, Utah. I was to be sworn in on the 28th of June. On the next day, I signed my John Henry and was sworn in, along with about 20 other nondescript characters. We were immediately shipped off to San Diego, California, to the Naval Training Center for "boot" training. Boot training was pretty much uneventful. I learned how to tell the front and back of a ship apart, swim, wash clothes, row a boat, march, and clean up a garbage dump, but not necessarily in that order.

After twelve weeks of "boots," I was sent to Norfolk, Virginia, to machinist's mate school. A machinist's mate in the Navy works in the bowels of the ship (engine room, boiler room, evaporators, etc.) when the ship is moving (under way) and cleans up the bowels when the ship is tied up to dock or at anchor (sitting still). I found out my chosen rate (profession) in the Navy was about the shittiest they could dream up. I didn't fit into navy life too well.

After I finished machinist's mate school in Norfolk, Virginia, I was sent to Yerba Buena Island, California (also called "Goat Island" or "Treasure Island"), which is located in the middle of the Oakland Bay Bridge. The Bay Bridge was practically new when I arrived there in April 1941. The one task I remember during my stay on Goat Island was driving the garbage truck for the island. Each morning I would get up about five a.m. and get my '38 Chevy dump truck and go over to the brig (jail) and pick up about four or five military prisoners, who would ride in the truck bed and empty the garbage cans into the dump bed of the truck. After we had made the rounds of the barracks and gathered all of the garbage, I would take the prisoners back to the brig. Then I would drive across the bridge to Pier 13 in San Francisco and dump the garbage into a garbage scow (the scow was a barge which would be towed out to the open ocean and emptied of the garbage). Can you imagine what the ocean floor outside the Golden Gate must look like after 150 years of crap being disgorged from the Navy barges?

On some of my liberties, in San Francisco and Oakland, I did some devilish things. Part of the time (from May 'til October 1941), I was stationed at Alameda Naval Air Station. I remember at times, when a bunch of us sailors would be up on the hills in Frisco late at night, with no money for a cab or even a streetcar (we were only getting $36 a month). We would walk along the street and look in cars for one with the doors unlocked. When we found an open car, we would all pile in and coast it clear down to Market or as close to where the liberty boat/bus destination would be.

Dare Keane Kibble (right) and two other sailors, taken in San Francisco in 1941, before the attack on Pearl Harbor.

Several times we almost had accidents at intersections because at times we would reach 40 or 50 miles an hour. I wonder if the cops ever figured out what was happening.

Another time, on a weekend, we met a couple of girls, who knew several other girls, who wanted to have a party. One of the girls lived with her parents on California Street (which is steep in places) in a three story house, the back of which opened out on the hill on all three floors. On this one particular Saturday, when the girl's folks supposedly were in Minnesota for two weeks, about eight of us sailors bought some beer and food for the party. We called the girls and were told to come on up. Well, the party proceeded until about two a.m., when sailors and girls were asleep everywhere, when the doorbell rang. The girl I was with was the daughter of the folks ringing the bell. In San Francisco, when you ring the doorbell in many homes, a person has to let the person(s) in by pushing another button to release the lock. The party was on the third floor which gave us about four minutes before the parents would reach the scene. I ran around waking sailors, telling them we had to get out the back door, but pronto. The girls were busy trying to clean up the mess. The sailors all started pouring out the back door.

In those days everyone received their milk in glass quart bottles at their doorstep, and wouldn't you know, there was about a dozen empty bottles sitting on the doorstep. The first guy ran right into the bottles and they started tumbling down the three flights of concrete steps to California Street. Needless to say, there were sailors scattering every which way.

★ ★ ★

About a week later, I went back to see the girl. Her father and mother looked me in the eye and told me I had better take good care of their daughter. I have often wondered if those parents knew I was one of the thundering horde present on the party night.

It was along about this time, June 1941, a friend of mine and I decided to take a week's leave and go home to Boise for a little R&R. We had to ride home with another gob (sailor) from our ship who had "Asiatic" service in the "Asiatic Fleet." We thought he was a little dingy from the China service. He had a 1932 Model B Ford sedan. It had a little V8 motor and, boy, a Model B was a nice little rig.

I had gone to school with the Asiatic sailor's sister. Boy, was she a pistol. It would take six good men and a mule to hog-tie the girl. I met her the other year (about 1970) and she was just like always, tougher-'n-nails and twice as rusty. She had been married about four times and "there ain't a man gud-enough" for her. I can imagine, like the old cowboy song says, "She could turn on a nickel and give you some change." Anyway, the Far East sailor was going to take about a month's leave, so we would have to find our own way back to the ship in Frisco.

When we arrived in Boise, my family (father, mother and sister (me brudder 'Moon,' my brother-in-arms whom I later met on Wake Island, at this time lived in the San Fernando Valley outside Los Angeles, California)) was very happy to see us as always. My father and mother were dirt poor and they drank too much, but the one magnificent characteristic I will always remember about them was their tremendous capacity for love. No matter where I roamed over the face of the earth, I always knew my parents loved me, and love is worth more than all of man's worldly possessions in this life. Love, love, love, there is nothing like it nor will there ever be.

My mother had bought my sister a Model A Ford 1930 roadster, with a rumble seat and wire wheels mounted with 6 x 16 inch tires. It was painted yellow and it was beautiful. She told me I could use it all the time I was on leave.

One night I managed dates for us with a couple of girls I had known in high school and during the summers I had spent in the Owyhee County. We took them up in the foothills of the Boise Front, along with some beer and food my mother prepared for us. We went up Rocky Canyon and over the summit into Barrel Springs. There were some nice flat grassy spots at Barrel Springs for picnicking in those days, but no more. It seemed my buddy decided my date should be his date, which was fine with me.

After several hours and mucho fried chicken and potato salad, I decided to turn the Model A around and pack up to go home. It was about one a.m. by now. However, when I tried to turn the car around, I ran into a dry wash and high-centered the frame. When I went to look for my buddy to help me dig the Ford out of its predicament, he was off somewhere with my date. I never was very hot stuff with the women, which was just as well, considering what was down life's trail in the near future.

Now, don't misunderstand. In those days, girls didn't bed down or shack up as readily as they do now. I think they call it "having a relationship" now. I still don't understand why they don't call it what it is. I suppose this generation is trying to paint a rosy picture or "make chicken salad out of chicken shit," as they say. In Alaska in my day, they called it "teepee creepin'," and stateside they called it "shackin'." Well anyway, nothing like that was going on in the mountains on that night so long ago.

Barrel Springs used to be on the old stage road on the way to Boise Basin in the old gold-rush days. My father drove a National Auto Stage up the Basin road in 1919 and 1920. It took two days for the round trip to Idaho City-Centerville-Quartzbury-Pioneerville-Boise City.

I dug the Ford off the high center with a tire iron by myself. I don't know of a tool God gave us which is more universal than the "old tire iron." As it happened, we didn't get back from the picnic until six a.m. the next day.

A couple of days later, we left to go back down to San Francisco. My sister took us out on Highway 30 (called Federal Way nowadays) and tearfully hugged and kissed me goodbye. She was still in high school. The next hug I would get from "Sis" would be five years later and a thousand miles down the road of life.

We decided to hitchhike down through Twin Falls and Elko, Nevada. The Winnemucca cutoff was not in existence in those days. Well, we got a ride to the junction of Highways 93 and 30. Three "turkeys" in a 1936 Ford Coupe stopped and offered us a ride into Twin Falls if we would ride in the trunk. We knew they had been drinking beer but such conditions didn't scare us, not in those days. We got in the trunk and the moment the car started, we knew we had pulled a faux pas. The driver started whipping the car back and forth across the highway trying to spook us, and he certainly succeeded. On about the fourth swerve, the driver lost control and the car started to roll, time and time again, down the barrow pit on the edge of the highway. My friend and I tried to hold on to the edge of the turtle back but eventually lost our grips. The force of gravity threw us both out of the car. When the car finally settled to a resting place on its top, my friend jumped up and started chasing the three "turkeys" with a boulder in hand. The three of them hightailed it down the highway with my friend on their tail. The last we saw of them, they were running across a hay field.

I had struck a large boulder with my hip. The hip started to swell with a knot about the size of my fist coming out on the hip bone. Both of our uniforms were filthy. Luckily, we were wearing our blues so the dirt didn't show so badly. We knew we had to get back to the ship by the next evening. The skipper had told us there would be no extensions, no matter what. When I tried to walk, the hip was very painful so a passerby said he would take us about three miles into Gooding to the hospital.

The people at the Gooding Hospital put me through an extensive examination and x-rayed my body several times. The doctor said I had ruptured a number of large blood vessels in my hip area. He didn't think anything serious would happen due to the rupture unless some blood clots started floating around in my system. He advised me to stay at the hospital for a few days and rest where they could monitor the swelling. I thought about the rage of the skipper and thanked the people for their wonderful care. And they didn't charge me a cent. Can't you just see one of our hospitals in this day and age passing out this type of humanitarian aid? My friend let me lean on him and we walked to the main drag (Highway 30) out of town. We hitched a ride from there clear to the junction of east-west 30 at Wells, Nevada, arriving at about 0500 the next day.

We were hungry and dead tired and my hip was killing me. We sat there quite a while until a new, white Lincoln Zephyr (1941) sedan picked us up. You might wonder how I remember the car, well, if you have ever seen a new Lincoln Zephyr, you would remember the scene with stark lucidity. The man was a construction worker in rebar and was going to San Francisco. He said he would have us there by evening before 2400 when our leave was up. What a break!

Well, the ol' boy kept the Zephyr rolling between 90 and 100 all the way into Reno. He had someone he had to see in Reno, so he let us out and told us he would be back in a while. He said he would pick us up in the spot where he let us out. I was positive he would never show up again but he met us exactly when he said he would. My friend and I had a couple of beers and something to eat. I remember the city had a beautiful water fountain and we practically took a bath in it. It was a warm summer day and the water felt so good, we were delighted to be alive.

Our "patron saint" (so to speak) arrived right on time. We climbed in the Zephyr and motored on down to San Francisco arriving well before 2400 hours. The man even drove us right to shipside at the dock, for by then I couldn't navigate too well on my hip. My friend helped me on board and I turned into sickbay the next morning. I was well in a couple of days and the skipper was mad as hell at me for getting bashed up on leave. So what was new?

The encounter with the "patron saint" did not end on the San Francisco dockside but on one dismal day in the winter of 1943, in Woosung, China, in a prison camp. I was walking along the compound road amongst thousands of other prisoners, trying to get some exercise, when I passed a man who sparked a shimmer of recognition. I spent the next several weeks trying to remember where I had known the man. He was about forty years old with lots of gray and I knew there was something about the eyes which looked so familiar. Well it finally came to me, this man in prison was the same man who gave me a ride across the Nevada desert one summer morn so long ago.

Anyhow, as soon as my memory made the compute, and during evening hours, I hunted for my benefactor. I finally found him. I couldn't believe how the last two years had beaten this man down, he had aged fifteen years. Maybe I had also. Anyhow, I walked up to him and asked if he remembered giving a couple of sailors a ride across the Nevada desert to San Francisco in the summer of 1941. He said, "Yes." I thought he would fall over when I told him I was one of those young men, and afterwards we became friends. I can't remember his name, but I will always remember him. God bless him wherever he is.

CHAPTER 2

Leaving Home

While we were still in the San Francisco area, eight of us sailors bought a 1931 Studebaker which was a black four-door sedan which could seat eight people (limousine). It was a real pleasure to ride in, with the mohair upholstery and lights everywhere. We paid 80 dollars for it. Each of the eight owners paid one dollar a month.

On each Monday we would draw by lot and each of the eight owners would get the car one day a week (one of the guys didn't drive). We had to pay so much a mile for gas and oil. I remember spending many a wonderful night in the old Studdee. Anyway, when our ship went to Pearl Harbor in October 1941, we left the Studdee parked on Market Street in San Francisco. We later received a letter from Traffic in San Francisco stating we owed them several hundred dollars in fines and penalties. One of us wrote a letter and enclosed the title and keys, stating we were giving the Studdee to the city as a gift in hopes the coming generations would remember us for it.

One other assignment handed me, before I went aboard ship for good, was building submarine nets at the old Tiburon Coaling Station in San Francisco Bay. In the days of the coal-burning ships before the days of fuel oil boilers, there was a huge coal yard at Tiburon, California, and the ships docked there to take on coal.

The Navy had taken over two riverboats, the Delta King and Delta Queen, which previously were used to run up and down the Sacramento River with passengers. We lived on the Delta King in staterooms and had the life of Riley except we had to work like hell every day, building the nets. The idea was to build these huge nets which would be stretched across the entrance to the San Francisco Bay to keep the foreign subs out. It would be provided with a gate which would be handled by a tug and opened to let ships in and out.

When we left Tiburon, I went to the shipyards in Oakland, California, to commission the USS *Tangier*. The *Tangier* was a seaplane tender and would take me to Puget Sound in Washington State and then on to Pearl Harbor. The skipper of the *Tangier* later knew the Navy would never be the same under my capable hands... he told me so personally.

While in Oakland, I did meet Wendell Willkie, the Republican candidate for the presidency. If my father had known I shook the hand of Wendell Willkie, he would've shot me before the Japanese had the chance.

While on the USS *Tangier*, I had a chief machinist's mate whom I'll call "Bozo." Bozo was in charge of the watch (work section) I had the misfortune to draw. He hated me and the feeling was mutual. It seemed Bozo was always on the shift ahead of mine which required my waking him for his tour in the engine room. When a ship is under way, the crew which operates the ship (during peacetime), is usually broken up into what is known as a "four on and eight off" watch cycle, which means a fireman or machinist will be on watch for four hours and off watch for eight hours. Of course, while you are not sleeping you still have to clean bilges, swab decks, etcetera, even though you're not on watch.

Well, Bozo had the nasty habit of going back to sleep after I had awakened him. Then, when he didn't show up for his watch, the watch officer would go get him. Naturally, he would say I had not awakened him, and the officer would always take a chief's word over a fireman's. Eventually, he was the reason for my volunteering, and I use the term loosely, for duty on an island in the far Pacific called "Wake."

Being on a naval ship is a horrible place to spend your youth. You are on a sheet of steel 24 hours a day. At night, or whenever the Navy decides you can sleep, you are folded in a space environment which resembles quadruple bunk beds, and at times quintuple, with the smell of oil and paint (or some shipmate's farts) continually in the air. Engines and motors are running 24 hours a day with the ship, and all it holds, vibrating continually. Then added to all this, you have some turkey in command who doesn't have enough sense to pour pee out of his hat.

The ocean can be rewarding and beautiful if you ever have the time to appreciate it. The one redeeming factor about navy life is cleanliness of your food and body.

When our ship left San Francisco Bay, in October 1941, we went to Bremerton, Washington, to take on a load of aerial torpedoes and planes for Pearl Harbor. When a ship is getting ready to move or weigh anchor, most of the men aboard have a certain task to perform before the ship is ready to sail (ships don't *sail* any more, they chug along powered by diesel, steam or nuclear-heated steam). The Navy uses all these archaic terms which are a carryover from the days of Columbus or the Egyptian Navy (i.e., barges). Once you teach a marine or sailor something, you can never get him to believe otherwise. The Navy uses a check-off sheet similar to a preflight check-off sheet in a modern commercial jet preparing for takeoff. Each ship has a siren and whistle which it uses in emergencies or fog. My task prior to getting under way was to go up in the stack and test the whistle and siren. When I had tested them and made sure they were operable, I was to call the bridge (same as a cockpit or center of operations) and tell them they're clear.

The ship was all ready to get under way for Pearl Harbor from Bremerton and the weather was quite foggy. When the command came over the intercom to "prepare to get under way, man your stations," I was told by a shipmate I had a special delivery letter waiting for me in the ship's mail room.

I had an idea it was from a dolly I knew in Oakland, California.

So I decided the *Tangier* would wait on me and proceeded to go stand in the mail line (in the Navy you have to stand in line for every occasion, even to die during battle) to get the special delivery letter. I guess I had been in line about twenty minutes, when another shipmate came by and said Chief Bozo was hot on my tail and mad as hell.

Soooo, I beat a hot path up to the bottom of the stack funnel. The funnel on a ship has a ladder inside and also has the stack, which houses the particulates and smoke from the firebox. When you stand at the bottom of the funnel you can usually see up to the sky and the funnel may be several stories high, depending on the size of the ship. There are several little platforms at intervals which a person can stand on and not be seen from the bottom or the top. When I looked up the funnel after climbing about halfway up, I could see the Chief coming down, so I just stepped off on one of the platforms and let him go by. Bozo was so mad he must have been blind for he passed within six inches of me and didn't even see me when he went by. I almost burst out laughing but thought better of it. Then I proceeded to go on up and clear the whistle and siren. I then called the bridge and reported "all clear."

Later on, Bozo blew his gut out telling me off, but I swore I did exactly what I was supposed to only I didn't tell him, or the captain later on, I was a little slow in doing it. The captain of the ship and I got so we were on a first name basis, with me being at captain's mast so often (captain's mast is equivalent to judicial court in civil law).

My father was the foreman at a Dodge garage in Boise for about fifteen years, starting in the '20s, and had taught me a lot about engines and automobiles. I could take any of them apart and put them back together before I joined the Navy. Consequently, I was continually assigned to small-boat duty when at anchor. The Navy uses small boats for any task which a cumbersome ship cannot perform efficiently or practically.

I remember one time when I was running the crash boat (which was powered by two straight-eight Packard engines and would do about 50-60 knots); I was reprimanded for racing with the big Pan Am Clippers during takeoff from San Francisco Bay. I still have a picture today of the *Tangier* with the crash boat on the stern.

Another experience which convinced me I would never make admiral was the "officers' wardroom supply" deal. One day at Pearl Harbor, I was doing small-boat duty, running the gobs and supplies between shore and the ship, when we were sent to get a load of officers' wardroom supplies. We were tied up at the dock and the supplies were being passed from the dock to the small boat. I happened to be the guy in the boat who was supposed to catch the supplies as the coxswain heaved them to me.

Well, he threw me a large box of razor blades and I missed catching the box, and where do you suppose the box went? Right, it went in the briny deep, at which spot the harbor was supposed to be about 100 feet deep. Do you know what the coxswain said I should do? He said I should dive for the box, and I told him to go do an impossible sex act.

Well, we shoved off from the dock and went back to the ship. The lieutenant in charge of the officers' wardroom was checking off the supplies as we handed them aboard ship and, of course, he missed the razor blades. He said, "What happened to the carton of razor blades?" I explained what had happened. He said "Kibble, your explanation is not acceptable." I told him if he wanted those razor blades, he could send in a request for a navy diver to go get them. He told me I "had" to produce the blades because they were paid for by officers' funds, and he wouldn't request a diver because such a request would throw the blame on him.

I told him those blades were gone and he could do anything he wanted to concerning them except they weren't coming out of my pay. I told him "the next time the officers wanted razor blades, let them go get them." And, of course, I had to go explain my actions and attitude to the captain at captain's mast the next day. After I explained what had happened, I never heard anything else about it. To this day, I still don't know what happened.

Another experience which assured my early retirement from the USS *Tangier* occurred while we were under way from the States to Pearl Harbor.

I had the "evaporator watch." The ships at sea make their own water by using the turbine's exhaust steam to heat sea water to the boiling point and then condense the resulting steam into water. The critical point in the operation is to leave a tiny bit of minerals and salt in the water so it resembles the water people are used to when acting as a civilian ashore.

Well, I checked all of my gauges and they seemed to be doing fine, making tons of acceptable water. Then I decided to go down to where a friend of mine was tending the main steam boilers.

After we had talked about 30 minutes, I went back to check on my "evaps" and as soon as I saw the gauges, I knew I was going to see my old friend the captain. I had made a huge tank full of contaminated seawater and dumped it into some fresh water tanks. After an eternity, I subdued the system and settled down to making "good" water so when my relief watch came on, I didn't say anything.

Of course, in the morning, breakfast was ruined and the whole crew was pissed when they showered or tried to wash clothes. They called all four of the "evap" watch crew to mast. I was the embodiment of innocence and knew there was no way the captain could prove guilt. In addition, of the four, there was one guy who was a bigger screw-up than I was, if possible. They were ready to nail him. Anyway, I couldn't let him take the rap for what happened so I 'fessed up, and went to see my friend, the guy who ran the boat.

I remember how balmy and wonderful Pearl Harbor and the Islands were in those days. There were only about 25,000 people, besides servicemen, in Hawaii. When the ship was tied up to the dock or at anchor in the harbor, we would sleep on the weather deck under the stars. What a wonderful couple of weeks in my life. I can remember walking along Waikiki Beach with only a few people in sight. The tallest building in town was the Royal Hawaiian Hotel. I would find myself wishing those days would never end, during those beautiful nights under the starlit skies.

The wind would blow, ever so gently, on your face and body and, at this moment, you knew this must be what the Lord's heaven will resemble when you enter the Promised Land. It would be a terrible shock to me, when I returned, again, to this heavenly land in September 1945, to see how man can totally ruin such a paradise in four short years.

Around November 1, 1941, there was a notice placed on one of the bulletin boards on the ship, saying a few volunteers were needed for expeditionary forces on some of the islands through-out the Western Pacific (Palmyra, Johnson, and Wake). A friend of mine, W.C., and I planned on buying a couple of motorcycles. The only problem being we didn't have the money saved and probably wouldn't have if we stayed around Hawaii. So we decided to volunteer for some far out island duty and save our money. After a year (when the island duty was to terminate) we would meet back at Pearl and take 90 days' leave.

We planned on going to the States, buying Harley '61s (which had the first overhead valves, as I remember) and zoom through the homeland like a couple of vagabonds. So we put in our requests.

From then on, my life took the most bizarre turn any person could ever anticipate.

CHAPTER 3

War of the Innocent

Old men are too wise to settle differences through open conflict. Young men of today will not listen to their elders; else many of their problems would be insignificant. Young men are too gullible to dispute what the leaders of the country tell them. So the young less-fortunates go off to give their lives to protect the wealthy, who stay home and reap the multitude of spoils.

During this period of time (1940-41) in the Pacific Theater, the great military geniuses of the United States decided it would be wise, from a strategic standpoint, to form what they called a "Defense Battalion" for each one of the outlying islands. This would protect the western flank of the Hawaiian Islands, or slow the enemy down enough to enable Pearl Harbor or Midway to ready themselves for invasion. Each of these islands was several thousand miles from nowhere.

A defense battalion contained about 400 marines. It was comprised of searchlights, communications, five-inch shore batteries, three-inch anti-aircraft guns, .50 caliber machine guns and .30 caliber machine guns. And of course, like the gyrenes[1] always say, each marine is actually a basic infantry person. Also, a number of fighter aircraft were to be attached to the island fortresses.

Well, the men to go to each island were chosen by lot from the volunteer naval personnel. I was chosen to go to Wake Island (and incidentally, my friend W.C. never went anyplace).

A person may wonder why the Navy would assign a machinist's mate to go to an island, when the only contingent who would be on the island would be marines and some aircraft. Well, our ship (the *Tangier*) was a seaplane tender. The *Tangier* supposedly would go to sea and act as a refueling and support ship for a squadron of long-range patrol seaplanes (PBYs, "Patrol Bombers" built by Consolidated out of San Diego).

The ship had everything on it to supply the planes or repair them, including: fuel, ammo, parts, bombs, etcetera. The Navy, at this time, was trying to recon or spy on the Marshall Islands (which belonged to Japan) with the help of the PBYs out of Pearl. The planes had to refuel at Midway but still could not reach the Marshalls so the Navy decided to send a refueling boat to Wake. This boat could be used to refuel the planes at night, offshore under the cover of darkness, without being observed by the watchful eyes of the Japanese subs. Well, I was to be the guy who operated and maintained the engine on the 60-foot refueling boat which had a tank amidships capable of holding 3,000 gallons of fuel.

So, the boat and four sailors (myself, Boatswain's Mate Binny, and two deck hands) were out aboard the USS *Wright* at Pearls for the trip to Wake Island. We sailed and arrived at Wake circa November 26, 1941, and that was one ship's sailing I should have missed.

Wake Island is a coral atoll. It was produced by little forms of life which die and clutch each other in a bear hug to become coral which in character reminds me of the lava rock we have in Idaho, only it's white. The highest point on the island is about 20 feet in altitude and there is no fresh water. There were thousands of gooney birds and no trees, only shrubs. Wake is actually composed of three islands: Wake, Peale, and Wilkes. I used to go swimming every day in the lagoon and watch the beautiful, small fish life. The island chain is about ten miles or so around and, at spots, you can almost throw a stone across the width. My life seemed to be quite serene, with taking care of the boat and the refueling tasks along with swimming.

The islands of Wake, Peale and Wilkes surround a beautiful lagoon. I don't remember how deep the lagoon was in the center, but in most places you could see the bottom with no trouble. When you looked down into the lagoon you could see every color imaginable. We kept the refueling boat (our boat) tied up to a dock on the lagoon side of the island of Wake, right next to Camp One (Marine Camp). Just a matter of feet from where the refueling boat was tied up, the contractors had built a channel to the south side of Wake, so when we went to refuel the PBYs, we went out the channel and on out to sea. We refueled the planes about a mile off the island. The shape of all the coral islands in the Pacific is almost the same. There will be a U-shaped island with a coral reef guarding the opening in the "U", therefore they call this type of island an atoll. The contractors had to dig the channel because it was almost impossible to cross the reef, which was on the northwest side of the island.

When we were working around the boat in the wonderful, south-sea balmy weather, we would on impulse jerk our clothes off and dive into the lagoon. When you were underneath the surface you could see a myriad of beautiful fish. Several times when we were going out to sea in a boat for some reason, we would take along a big hunk of meat and with the aid of a huge hook and line, fish for whatever we could catch. Most of the time we would hook into a shark, which we never ate; in fact, we never ate any of the fish we caught. Normally, they were so big they would straighten out the hook. Many times, when refueling the PBYs (which would take about an hour), we and the plane's crew would go for a skinny dip around the boat and plane; those were the days.

When I look back at those days, in my memory bank, it seems I was not even cognizant of what was going on around me. For instance, I don't recollect wondering or questioning either myself or anyone else, as to why the PBYs were wandering around down in this part of the South Pacific, below the equator, with bombs on their wings and ammo in their guns.

I knew practically nothing about the status of world affairs concerning the Japanese, nor did I realize how close I was to Japan (I was 400 miles closer to Tokyo than I was Honolulu), nor did I seem to care. I knew from my study of geography about where most of the main land masses or islands in the Far East were in relation to the Pacific Ocean, but outside of this skiff of knowledge, it seems I was in total bliss.

As I look back, I believe the politicians and media had lured me into a sense of absolute security as a citizen of the United States, for "no one would dare attack this great nation of ours," and "our armed forces were invincible," and if you dared question the strength of the nation, either morally or economically, you were labeled a "Nazi-lover" or some other contemptuous adjective. Just before we were sworn into the U.S. Navy, "they" showed us a film picturing ten or twelve battleships, all abreast, plowing through the beautiful Pacific Ocean, which was enough to indicate the unbeatable nature of our armed forces.

A large Boise, Idaho construction company was a civilian contractor on the island. Some of the civilians went to Wake to secure exemption from the draft into the many armed forces, others to earn big bucks. Fate turned the tables on them. Recently, through their lobbying efforts they have been granted a status putting them on par with the servicemen of Wake, with an honorable discharge and all the trimmings. Of course, they asked for and received their civilian pay all the time they were overseas and in prisoner of war camps.

Such actions as these do not necessarily endear my country to me.

WHICH ENEMY?

I volunteered my life as a warrior

The battle not recognized

The enemy was not apparent

'Til Jesus opened my eyes

— dkk

My observations and experiences during the next four years of my life caused me to question the values and substance of the morals and mores to which society had indoctrinated me in the previous years of my life.

During and after my prisoner-of-war (POW) days, it seemed I was always standing on the sidelines watching the human stream meander through life, making the same tragic errors which have been made by civilization after civilization from time unknown.

Humans are not capable of guiding their own destiny and if they are ever to succeed to a higher plane of existence, they must practice a set of laws, even though they believe it spells their doom, which are predicated on loving grace and no other basis.

CHAPTER 4

The Sinner

Would that I could somehow look

My Savior in the eye

To Him my life's an open book

Oh! What a sinner am I!

— dkk

I believe there are only two moments in a person's lifetime when it may (and I say "may" with tongue in cheek) be possible to be a true follower of Jesus Christ.

One being when he is very young, with very little indoctrination from humans in the society, and the other is when he's very old and in the short rows of death, at which time he or she is devoid of any earthly values except unconditional love.

Persons of third and fourth world countries are very much closer to God and true happiness than any persons in the more highly civilized nations of the world. These peoples are practically devoid of any earthly possessions and yet if you give them a momentary ration of food, you will note a serenity settle into their existence.

On Monday, the 8th of December, 1941, I got up in the morning, ate breakfast and went down to work on the bowser-boat (the tank in the middle of the gas refueling boat was called a "bowser" or "bowzer").

During the morning, we heard some scuttlebutt (rumors) which indicated the Japanese had bombed Pearl Harbor. We noted some of the aircraft fighters had taken off. Also, we noted that the marines were in their gun positions. We had received no notification or orders from our officers whatsoever, so we continued our work at the boat dock.

At noon, we all jumped in a ton-and-a-half stake truck and headed up Wake Island (as opposed to Wilkes or Peale), past Camp One (which was where the marines were housed), past the airstrip and were headed toward Camp Two (which was the civilian camp where we were housed and fed). There were about 400 marines, 60 sailors, 10 army, and 1400 civilians on the island.

The sequence of events which occurred on Wake Island during the next sixteen days are detailed to some extent by the following log of an officer who wrote them down and smuggled the epistle through four years as a prisoner of war of the Japanese (1941-1945).[2]

> **Monday, December 8, 1941. 12:02 p.m.** . . . Today 26 Jap bombers (two engine type) bombed and machine-gunned Wake, killing 30 men and wounding several others. . . . Airfield hit the hardest both in men and planes. . . . Seven (of twelve)

of our fighters were bombed and burned on the ground. . . . Pan Air (PanAm) Hotel and facilities were also wiped out and killing ten employees. . . . The Clipper (Boeing flying boat) escaped damage and the personnel got off to Honolulu after the attack. . . . Thirteen contract (civilian) men killed . . .

Tuesday, December 9, 1941. . . . Three planes in order. . . . At 12:10 another raid of sixteen Jap planes. . . . Lt. Kliener and Hemmering Hank Elrod met them at approximately 11,000 ft. and downed one. . . . Three marines reported missing, (Hunt, Tucker, and Mitwalski) following the raid. Camp Two was heavily hit, the hospital was burned, but all patients were removed except three which were machine-gunned in their beds . . .

Wednesday, December 10, 1941. . . . Third raid of bombers at 10:20. . . . Approximately 16,000 ft. . . . one section coming back over Camp Two, doing bad damage. . . . Capt. Elrod downed two of them and the three-inch guns sent two away smoking . . .

Thursday, December 11, 1941. . . . All hell broke loose this morning. . . . Two Jap cruisers, five destroyers, and two transports began shelling the Island. . . . We managed to get three fighters into the air with two (100 lb.) bombs each. . . . (First hop, Capt. Elrod, C. Frenner, and C. Tharin) . . . . Our planes bombed and sank a cruiser and two destroyers. The five-inch coast guns got good hits on the other cruiser and one transport was sunk. . . . It was later reported that our subs sank all but one destroyer as they were making their escape. . . . Lt. Kliener reported that he bombed and machine-gunned a Jap sub. . . . Then Major Devereaux went up in a plane, and said that he saw an oil slick on the water so it is almost certain the sub sank. . . . At 9:30 p.m., seventeen Jap bombers came over at 20,000 ft. and Lt. Davidson shot down one. . . .

Friday, December 12, 1941. . . . At 4:15 a.m., one four-engine Jap bomber came over, dropping its load but did little damage. . . . Capt. Tharin came in on his tail and shot his hull full of holes and that two engines were on fire . . .

Saturday, December 13, 1941. No raid. . . .

Sunday, December 14, 1941. . . . At 3:40 a.m., one Jap patrol bomber dropped approximately seven bombs, no damage. . . . At 11:40 a.m., 37 Jap bombers at 20,000 ft. They did most of their damage on Camp One and the waterfront. One of our planes was burned on the ground . . .

Monday, December 15, 1941. . . . At 8:00 a.m., four Jap bombers dropped their load but no damage . . .

Tuesday, December 16, 1941. . . . At 1:40 p.m., 27 Jap bombers attacked Camp Two, hitting it fairly hard and also Camp One. . . .

Wednesday, December 17, 1941… (Apparently, there was no bomber and sea activity on this day) No entry on the log.

Thursday, December 18, 1941. . . . At 11:20 a.m., 27 heavy bombers hit again at the AA (anti-aircraft) guns but as usual doing very little damage. . . . Tredge and Bourguini (two pilots) went up and shot down three bombers after our AA guns had filled them full of holes. The AA brought down two . . .

Friday, December 19, 1941. . . . At 11:35 a.m., 36 heavy bombers came over in two flights of eighteen each. . . . 'V' formations. . . . Guns brought down four. . . . They flew at 24,000 ft. . . . the highest yet. . . .

Saturday, December 20, 1941. . . . A PBY U.S. Navy patrol bomber landed here at 6 p.m. . . . At 2:30 p.m., 27 Jap bombers came in at 19,000 ft. . . . They hit Camp Two and Peale Island hard. . . . Bombs were hitting close on Peale, missing all AA gun positions by mere feet. . . . Two buildings were burned, some ammunition lost by direct hit. . . .

Sunday, December 21, 1941. . . . The PBY left at 6 a.m. . . . At 9:40 a.m., 30 Jap dive bombers came in and made a 45-minute attack. . . . It was a very poor showing, very little damage. . . . Our planes took off during the raid but could not find their carrier. . . . They were too low for the AA's but machine guns gave them plenty worry. . . . At 12:25 p.m., 33 Jap bombers came in from the west. . . . They hit Peale and Camp Two. . . . Three barracks burned. . . . Direct hit on three AA guns on Peale, killing Sgt. Wright and wounding four others... Guns moved into coast defense position . . . .

Monday, December 22, 1941. . . . 12:35 p.m. to 1:05 a.m. . . . We were heavily shelled from Jap ships at sea . . .

Tuesday, December 23, 1941. . . . They ran two destroyers on reef to land on Wake at 3:00 a.m. . . . Small landing boats landed on Wilkes. . . . More destroyers, cruisers, and battle wagons showed up at dawn with several squadrons of dive bombers. . . . We surrendered at 8:00 a.m. . . . We lost 37 contract employees, ten Pan Air employees, 100 U.S. Marines and twelve planes (we only had twelve to start with).

The above does a fairly good job of describing the major events which happened during the Battle of Wake Island. However, it does not adequately describe how one sailor felt and responded to the confrontation.

When the Jap bombers hit the island on December 8th, I was in the back of a stake bed truck at the west end of the air strip, heading for Camp Two for lunch.

During the morning of the 8th, the boat crew (four men) and I had watched the Pan Am clipper take off for the island of Guam. As we were watching the plane, we noted he was dumping his fuel. We wondered exactly what this meant. At this time in my life, I didn't realize a long-haul plane can only land with so much of his take-off weight. As we watched, the pilot gently set the clipper down in the lagoon. One must remember, Wake Island is only the size of a small ranch (2000 acres or three square miles) and in some places, I could hit a golf ball from one side of the island to the other. In elevation, the island is about 20 feet high. When you are at sea, you can easily miss the island from a couple miles out.

The landing strip took up one third of the total land mass of the island.

The sky had been stuccoed with cumulus clouds all morning and we had watched four of our Grumman fighters take off on patrol. At exactly noon, as we were riding along in the stake truck on the airstrip, we looked up and saw all of these bombers coming in from the southwest. All at once we saw the flaming sun insignia.

Someone beat on the truck cab and told Mac (the driver) to stop. Incidentally, Mac (not his real name) was the craziest guy you would ever want as a wartime comrade-in-arms. The truck stopped and we all bailed out, with about five or six of us running single file in an easterly direction. By the time Mac had stopped the truck, we were at the eastern end of the landing strip.

Then all hell broke loose! The ass on the guy in front of me disappeared. It was completely blown away. I could hear and see the slugs hitting all around me along with fragmentation bombs. Then the guy behind me yelled and fell. I was scared shitless and knew I would be next. The planes on the strip were exploding and burning as I ran past them. I looked up at the bombers and knew I could see the gunners sighting in on me. If only those damn machine-gun slugs would stop whining and thudding. How in the hell did I ever get into this mess? Here I was on a spit of an island, in a war I knew nothing about, with death burning down my neck. My only thought was to run, run, run...

I was so damn scared because I never tried to adjust my mental tempo to anything as terrifying as this. I was just a 20-year-old sailor from Idaho, who was trained to fight on a ship, not dodge machine-gun fire on a desert island.

I had on a pair of moccasins and I know I was running the 100-yard dash in record time. By the time the first section of bombers had passed me, I had outrun all of the other guys and I sat down to look at my feet because they hurt like the devil.

As I ran out of the moccasins, the coral started cutting my feet with every step. They were bleeding quite badly. Eventually, I looked up to see the huge tank which was sheltering me from the roaming bombers and their nasty lethal dose of death. Lo and behold, it was a huge gasoline storage tank.

Feet or no feet, I left there pronto. By then the second wave of bombers were coming in from the northwest and I started back toward the airstrip, looking for a place of cover. By this time, I was gaining some sense of rational judgment. Any little old thing to hide behind (remember there are no trees on Wake, only bushes). By the road, I found a small ditch and dove into it.

This time the enemy planes were right on top of me but the bombers' gunners didn't see me. I thought "How could they help but see me?" I wished then I had some kind of weapon to fire at them. I was scared as hell but also mad as hell at not only the Nips but also at myself for letting such events enter my life.

Anyway, I didn't hear any slugs hitting the ground around me. War is the shits! Here I was sitting right in the middle of one and I still didn't know whether someone was shooting at me. I could hear guns firing everywhere. I was lying face up and happened to think "Do I want to take slugs in the front or the back?" I decided to turn over.

After the adjacent fireworks ceased, I watched the bombers fly into the clouds to the south. I then decided to tear my shirt into strips and wrap around my feet. As I was doing this, I saw our four fighter planes come into the island and turn in the direction the bombers had taken. I was to learn later, the fighters never did find the enemy bombers. Remember, these were the days before much radar. The bombers had left the airstrip in a mess. Planes were burning everywhere. Seven had been hit on the ground. There were guys bleeding everywhere.

I decided to walk toward Camp Two where my clothes were and see if I could get my sea bag, which had all of my earthly belongings in it. I needed to get some clothes, including a pair of shoes (my feet were really bleeding now), shirts, and a coat.

As I was walking along, I saw the Clipper take off, heading for the States. I remember wishing our PBY squadron (VP-22), to which I belonged, would drop by and pick me up. No such luck.

CHAPTER 5

Reality

As I came back to reality, a truck honked at me, and there was Mac in his green '41 Chevy stake wanting to know if I wanted a ride.

I asked him if he got hit. The nut said he had crawled under his truck when we bailed out at the airstrip, and not a slug had touched him or the truck.

To oscillate for a moment, in the late '30s, the U.S. had what was known as an "Asiatic Fleet." It was comprised of some old "four stacker" destroyers and cruisers, most of which were sunk right at the start of WWII by the Japs. We had a large contingent of sailors and marines in the Orient. The men who did duty in the Asiatic Fleet were known to be quite "worldly." While on duty there, they all lived a very high life due to the disparity between the U.S. dollar and the Chinese yen. They had apartments including beautiful live-in Eurasian dollies, the very best of food and liquor, and very little work. This supposedly compensated them for overseas duty in the Orient. Consequently, when one of these sailors was transferred back to the Pacific Fleet, they were about half nuts and their brain was alcohol- or opium-soaked. Thus was my friend "Mac." I understand he is still alive and lives in Florida somewhere. I remember Mac always loved to smoke Pall Mall cigarettes.

When Mac and I reached Camp Two, I found my barracks were burned to the ground along with my sea bag.

On circa December 9, 1941, I was "shanghaied" by the Marines and for the next four years was to fight, sleep, eat, work and exist with the Marines. In fact, I had more time in the Marine Corps than I did in the Navy. I don't remember the name of the officer to which I was enslaved. It seemed any marine officer who came along was authorized to give me any order he wished. I never knew who to report to, or who or which outfit I was fighting with.

You see these movies about how organized the Armed Forces are when they go into battle. How the privates report to the sergeants, the sergeants report to the first lieutenants, how the first lieutenants report to the captains, etcetera, etcetera, etcetera.

Well, wishful thinking is a far cry from the progression of a real battle (as opposed to a skirmish such as those fought in Desert Storm). They are the damnedest screw-up you can imagine. The communications are rotten, you don't know whether you are shooting at friend or foe, and don't care. You're still fighting the battle after you've been surrendered by someone whom you may have never seen. You never know when you will be out of ammo. The food always gives you the shits. One day you get five meals and then the next two days you get nothing. You never get enough sleep. Your body and clothes are filthy and remind you of the street people in New York City. Every guy who comes along gives you orders countermanding the orders you received five minutes earlier. Then, you're more apt to be wounded or killed by your own troops, "friendly fire," than you are "on purpose" by the enemy. And the list goes on, ad infinitum.

It seems on about December 9 at about dusk, someone came along (a marine officer) and said for me and another sailor to climb up the water tower. We were to keep a lookout for anything we might see concerning some presence, either on land or at sea. They had strung a field telephone line up to the water tower for communications. Where it went to, I was never told, all I knew was when I cranked the handle, some character answered on the other end. It may have been the Japanese for all I knew. Sounds like the Marine Corps, doesn't it?

As I said previously, there was no fresh water on the islands. All of the water was made from evaporators like the ones on the seagoing ships, then pumped up to the water tower for pressure to the user.

The first night, I remember, I covered half of the horizon and a guy I'll name "Dick" covered the other half, supposedly. About midnight, I went around to see how Dick was doing and you guessed it, he was asleep. I swung my pair of night binocs at him and hit him in the head. I didn't hit him hard enough to knock him out and he wanted to know why I hit him so hard. I told him this wasn't a game anymore, this was for real. I hinted strongly I wasn't going to give my ass to the Japs just so he could have his beauty nap and also, if I caught him asleep again, on watch, I would swing the binocs as hard as I could or else throw him off the tower. I didn't have a gun or I would have shot him. At the time, I couldn't recall when I had been so mad. I actually believe to this day, Dick really didn't realize what serious trouble he was in at the time. Needless to say, Dick didn't sleep the rest of our tour of duty on the water tower.

A couple days later, I was transferred to a machine-gun outfit, which ended my watch tower task. On one occasion, there was an air raid while I was going somewhere (I don't remember where right now) down through the brush. I was looking around for somewhere to spend the time during a bombing raid (the bombers petrified me every time they came over) when all of the sudden I came upon a marine.

The reason I mention this situation is to disclose the state of mind of even the supposedly "well-trained" combat marine during the thick of the battle. The marine was standing out in an open spot with a Thompson .45 cal. sub-machine gun, which was commonly called a "Tommy-gun." He was firing at the bombers which were several thousand feet in the air. This marine might as well have been throwing cotton balls at the planes for all the damage he was doing to the Nips on a certain day in December. So if the marines were this much confused, you can imagine the state of mind and soul of the few sailors, with no training and no officers or leadership of any kind.

It was about this time during the war, while I was up at Camp Two, doing something which I don't recall, when a navy officer came along in a truck and stopped to give the sailor with me and myself a task to do. He had several boxes of greenback bills he said we were to destroy because he didn't want the Japanese grabbing the money. We took the money off down towards the south beach and found a pile of ammo boxes which were supposed to be water-proof. We decided we wouldn't destroy the money and proceeded to stuff thousands of dollars into the ammo boxes. We didn't take time to count it. We thought someday, if this war ever ended and we were still alive, we'd come back and retrieve the money. Anyway, we buried it all by a big rock and by a big piling for a marker. I also had four paychecks from the Navy in Honolulu which I had been saving and carrying in my wallet. I tore them up, for I determined I could always ask the Navy to reissue the checks, provided I would ever again see the United States in this lifetime. Boy, what a miscalculation if there ever was one. After the war ended and I once again returned to the States, I did ask the Department of the Navy to pay me the wages they owed. I swear it almost took an Act of Congress to get the monies the great white father owed me.

At about this point in time, some marine officer sent me to the command post, where Major Devereaux was hibernating. I stayed there for a couple of days with nothing to do except pray during every bombing raid, hoping the bombs missed us, and they did. Psychologically, the bombing raids in the Command Post (CP) were terrifying, for you knew the enemy was trying to hit the CP. Bombing is worse than having someone shooting at you because the bombs are so damn erratic.

It may sound sadistic, but I honestly believe it would be very healthy for the U.S. to experience a bombing raid by an enemy, every couple of months in say 30 or 40 cities. Nothing will make you more "earthy" than to have a couple of 500-pound bombs land next door. We need to return to basics in this country.

Now, let's get back to the bombs falling. On the 11th of December, 1941, I was sent down to Camp One again, to man a machine gun. It was a .30 caliber, Browning water-cooled machine gun, and shot about 600 rounds a minute. This would have been fine except the only machine gun I had seen was in the show *Sergeant York* with Gary Cooper. The gunnery sergeant who gave another sailor (whom I'll call Moon) and I our five minute course in gunnery said we were to shoot in bursts and to take the breach apart if we had a "jam while firing." He forgot to tell us how to do this operation. They gave us our gun, two boxes of ammo, and about five empty burlap bags. The "Sarge" then told us to go back in the bush toward the lagoon and set up.

Now remember, we had only the gun, ammo and sacks. No bedding, no clothes, no food or water, and no shovel. And we had never shot a machine gun before. I told Moon, who was from Los Angeles, he could be the gunner and I would carry the ammo. He said "bullshit," and let me know he had never fired a gun before except to qualify in boot camp on a .30 caliber Springfield rifle.

Well, when I was a youngster (I was all of 20 years now), I had done a great deal of hunting with all different kinds of guns. So I decided I would feel better relying on myself, facing the enemy, than trusting Moon. It's kind of like driving a car; you feel safer when you are in the driver's seat than when you're a passenger. If you must be committed, be committed to yourself.

Moon and I sat down about 200 feet off the lagoon side of the road which ran from Camp One to the airstrip. We decided we needed a few necessities in order to survive, such as a few tools, a couple of mattresses, some water and one-hell-of-a-lot more ammo. The boxes only held 250 rounds. So Moon took off and was gone a while. He then returned with two mattresses which, incidentally, later on were to probably save our lives. Later, Moon found some water and hardtack (which is flour baked in a cookie form and can be used for knee pads while playing football) and some tools. . . . Moon later on found where the marines had a big cache of ammo. The marines made sure they weren't going to run out of ammo. Every time you turned around, you were amazed by the "bravery" shown by these stalwart defenders of freedom.

Anyway, Moon purloined about 10,000 rounds of .30 cal ammo for us, which we hid in the bush. I'm not sure, but Moon may have been a second-story man (a burglar who enters from the second floor) in civi-life.

The next day, we were able to get some shovels and fill the sandbags. We stood the sandbags in a stack and placed the machine gun on top so we could fire at low-flying aircraft. Those same sandbags, later on, were to save our lives.

You are probably wondering why we scrounged around for some mattresses. Well, the highest point on Wake Island was 20 feet above sea level. This altitude translated into, digging two feet under the ground (coral), you normally would be standing in seawater. So, you couldn't dig a decent foxhole to hide in during bombing raids. Remember the ground area which you had available for playing hide and seek with the enemy was only about the size of a dairy farm. And you always had about 20 or 30 bombers looking for you. If the bombers took pictures, which they did every day, and you were out where they could see you, the next day you could expect a load of bombs on your front porch. I may sound flippant about the whole thing now, but bombs are the most disheartening weapon in any arsenal. They scared the living daylights out of me every time I heard those engines droning overhead.

Anyway, Moon and I calculated we could dig a hole until we hit seawater and then lay down in the hole and pull a mattress over the top of us. Thus, the bomb would have to get a direct hit or we would be protected from most shrapnel. Most of the people killed by bombs are killed by perimeter blasts and shrapnel, not by the bomb blast itself.

You must remember, in the 23 days during which Wake Island held out against the Japanese, we had approximately 300 bombers, not counting the dive bombers from the aircraft carriers, drop their loads on us. They always hit one or two targets: either the area around Camp Two or the airstrip and area around Camp One (Moon, Kibble & Co. were a short distance east of Camp One). We had bomb craters everywhere you could glance.

CHAPTER 6

Buried Alive

Did you know you can hear the bomb coming which is going to kill you?

Around noon on December 18, Moon and I heard the bombers coming in on their daily milk run so we lay down in the little trench and pulled up the mattresses over us. Then lo and behold, we heard this whistling sound coming right for us and we both knew we were going to die. When it hit, the concussion threw us both about four or five feet in the air, and when we dropped back to the earth Moon started yelling his back was on fire. What had happened was the blast had sent a red hot piece of shrapnel under Moon while we were up in the air. After Moon's initial yell we felt a tremendous weight on top of us. I believe we were both unconscious for a matter of time, how long a time I don't know. But after a while, I was on my side facing Moon's ass end and we started talking. We could not lift the mattresses nor could we see daylight. We could breathe from the air pocket made between the mattresses and our bodies. Then after what seemed like an eternity, we decided we were buried at the edge of the bomb crater by the earth the bomb had displaced. In other words, we were buried alive by a 500-pound bomb. We were sure, in a few moments, we would suffocate, and rightly so.

What we didn't know was a few marines under a gunnery sergeant happened upon our gun position. They were walking up the road after the planes left, and, looking at the devastation the bombing caused in Camp One, decided to come over and see if the bombs had hit any guns or troops. . . . When they arrived, they found the gun, which wasn't touched by the blasts, but they couldn't find us. They started looking around. We could hear "Gunner" yelling at the marines, and saying he knew there were some sailors around this gun somewhere (I can still hear his booming voice). He was a Dane or a Norwegian or from that part of the world. He also was one good marine and I really grew to like him in the next four years. I read a while back of his death.

When the marines came close enough for Moon and I to hear them, we started yelling as loud as we could, with the air which was left in our temporary tomb.

Well, "Gunner" heard us and started digging as fast as he and the other marines could with no shovel available. They finally pulled us out of our "nest" and then they bandaged Moon's back. He had an ugly burn. I guess the shrapnel of a bomb is several thousand degrees when it explodes. Sooooo, I figured those two mattresses saved our lives.

★　★　★

BURIED ALIVE

It was about this time during the Wake War, when a couple of civilians took off in a 27-foot whaling sailboat for Australia and were never heard from or seen again. With the Nips bombing Pearl Harbor and the strength of their air power we were witnessing, the present inhabitants of Wake Island pretty well knew what the outcome of this fracas was going to be.

The boat crew, of which I was a part, who brought the 60-foot refueling boat to Wake, all gathered together one night in the bush to determine whether we might fill the 3000-gallon tank, which was on the boat, with diesel fuel and load the cabin, which was in the bow, with water and food, and take off for North or South America, whichever one we might hit first.

We calculated we would have enough fuel for over 6000 miles. The boat was constructed of fine wood and was exceptionally seaworthy, and I had plenty of spare parts for the engine and bilge pumps. We could put my .30 caliber machine gun on the bow for some protection, although not much, if we ran into a Nip sub or aircraft, but beggars can't be choosers.

Bilge pumps are needed during storms to pump the water out of the bottoms. Sixty feet sounds like a long, large boat but when you're on the ocean in a storm, it looks and feels like a paper cup.

We talked over the pros and cons. If we could make it to the Americas and the island had surrendered, we would be heroes. If we made it to the Americas and the island had held off the Japanese, we would be court-martialed. If we didn't make it to the Americas, it wouldn't make any difference.

As it turned out, I wish now we had taken the chance and tried to make the trip. I would never, ever go through the hellish years of the rest of World War II just to continue my life.

THE SILVER MISTRESS

When the sparkling Mistress

Of the ocean night,

Lured man to sail

In the nocturnal light.

Oh, why did we pause

To depart from hell,

For our Mistress was calling

To bid the island farewell.

In the years to come

We would regret our choice,

Oh, why wasn't the call

Of our Mistress' voice

Covered with silver

From Neptune's hand,

Bidding us come

To a faraway land.

— dkk

We knew we could float down the channel which led out of the lagoon to the open sea with the tide tonight and no one would be the wiser. It was a beautiful night with the moon playing peek-a-boo in the big, billowy clouds. We could wait and hit the channel when the moon went behind a huge cloud. By running under full power from the diesel engine, we would be a couple miles at sea before the moon came out again. The marine guard at the channel would never hear us with the breakers on the island shore roaring continually.

In those days, men were blown to bits and no one missed them. Everyone was worried about their own skin. Yes, and the brave marines, too. No one really knew who we (the navy men) were, for the naval officers in charge of us, had all disappeared (God knows where they went) and we never saw them again.

Anyway, we voted against the trip, and as if to seal our decision and doom, a 500-pound bomb landed directly dead-center on our boat the next day.

Within the first few days of the war, the island command had a number of bulldozers (driven by civilian contractors) bury almost all the canned food and any type of food which was not perishable. They tried to place water in cans all along the main road.

There was practically total chaos as far as any organized fighting machine, except for the marines, and they did everything half-assed. The marines were trained in the discipline of battle, although their units were broken into groups with poor or no communications.

To me, the heat of battle seemed like a bizarre world of fantasy, in which I could withdraw anytime I felt like it. I absolutely could not believe the United States would place us in such a compromising position with absolutely no defense. I had no training whatsoever in battlefield discipline . . . no training on weapons . . . no clothes to wear in battle . . . no idea what to do for food or water . . . and no sidearms (pistols or rifles) to use against the enemy infantry.

I had been trained on how to repair diesel engines . . . how to run a machine shop . . . and how to pull a watch in an engine room aboard ship when under way.

What in the hell was I doing on a machine gun, on a tiny island in the western Pacific (the name of which I had never even heard of until four weeks ago)?

Really what I needed more than anything, was training in how to control my temperament and how to face the fact I was here and there was nothing in God's world I, nor any other "man," could do about it. How should I conduct myself on this little part of the world in which I was positive I would spend the last few days of my life?

Moon and I kept discussing what to do in case the enemy landed on the island and overran our gun position. We knew nothing about hand-to-hand combat. We didn't even have a knife.

By the way the battles were going, we could deduce we were going to lose the island, especially after the battle of December 11th in which the Japanese committed a number of capital naval ships. Also, the Japanese had attacked with their naval dive bombers which meant aircraft carriers were somewhere off the island waiting to pounce on our tiny spit of land when the high command gave the word. We knew the Japanese would not send a carrier task force on this mission without extensive backup.

What we didn't know was the Japanese high command were convinced the fortifications, troops, aircraft and weaponry were of such force, based on the resistance met to date, they decided to pull some of the task force headed to Midway down to our section of the Pacific to clobber our pathetic defense force.

And if the foregoing wasn't enough to paint a gloomy picture, almost everyone on the island had dysentery from eating out of cans and drinking water out of any container available. Even finding a roll of toilet paper was almost an impossibility.

It seemed I had never felt so helpless in my whole life. I knew I was going to die in the battle which was coming as sure as the sun would come tomorrow. And then I wondered if I would be brave enough to fight to the end or would I turn into a whimpering coward. The men who had already gone to meet their Lord seemed to have a contented look on their face. To the coming generations who read this story, maybe not when but if they read this story, please realize fighting a war in this manner is a tough way to settle differences. It is much easier to be in an airplane or on a ship rather than down in the bush bare-handed.

Needless to say, I prayed almost constantly to my God, as I knew Him at this time. I had to pinch myself continually to make sure this was the real thing. I figured out what the odds were whereby I should be here in this predicament rather than some other "brave" citizen. My chances were about 100,000 to one.

BURIED ALIVE

I notice today, since the advent of the intercontinental ballistic missiles, our stalwart politicians and the wealthy of this country have decided, due to the proximity of death and destruction, to not have any global conflicts and only incorporate small brush wars in their discharge of foreign policy and the monopoly of the world economy.

CHAPTER 7

The Beach

On the 20th of December, a PBY patrol bomber came to the island and landed in the lagoon. It was attached to VP-22, the squadron to which I was attached. I thought for a while maybe they would pick up the boat crew and take them back to Pearl Harbor on their return. I didn't know it then but they had already written us off as expendable. They were here to pick up some army major in Intelligence and return him to Pearl Harbor. Screw the peons. The PBY took off the next morning without us. You can't imagine how depressing it was to see the plane disappear into the clouds in the eastern sunrise over the water. In watching the clouds envelop the plane, I felt the umbilical cord tethering me to my family and country disintegrating.

On the 21st of December, the marine command decided they would put our machine gun and crew (along with two other gun crews like ours, including two sailors per .30 cal) down on the beach. Our commission was to frustrate and impede the Japanese landing parties as long as we could stay alive. We were to stop the first wave of the enemy to land at this point on the island. We were directly opposite Camp One on the ocean side, or southern beach, of the island. We had another .30 cal. gun crew on our left, about 300 or 400 yards away, and another on our right, the same distance.

The civilians took a dozer and built us a bomb shelter on the beach with beams and coral stacked on top. You had to crawl down in and lay on your belly but it would hold all of the navy crew who was on the beach. We were to stay in the shelter during air attacks.

We knew what was in store for us. The marines (bless their brave souls) were back in the bush. They said they would back us up. The marines, after we were overrun and annihilated on the beach, thought they would have a chance if the Navy could soften the Nips' advance. I hope nobody tries to tell me ever again how brave the marines are.

During the early morning hours of the first night on the beach, Moon and I were huddled behind our five sandbags with our machine gun. Also, Moon had gone on an arms scouting trip and picked up a box of hand grenades to use as sidearms, which would be better than nothing. You can imagine how long 500 rounds of .30 caliber would last chomping through a weapon which fired 600 rounds a minute, during a frontal assault by the Nips.

That night out of nowhere, from up the beach, a .50 cal. machine gun opened up, firing down the beach in our direction. Some of the slugs hit our sandbags and as usual the great marine communication system told us nothing about the guns being there. Moon and I knew if we allowed them to keep firing, in no time the .50 cals would chew their way through our sandbags. So, I turned our .30 cal and started spraying the site of the muzzle blast of the .50

cal. They stopped firing immediately. Since then, I know they were firing to clear their guns and were afraid to fire over the water because the Nips would spot their position.

I can't explain how much of a mental lift I received from firing the gun. It seemed to mesmerize me and something sparked inside of me.

However, in about an hour, a marine captain and his squad of brave marines came down to our position, and ordered Moon and I to come to attention. He then asked who was firing the gun and I said, "You're looking at him." At which moment, he knocked me down with his fist. When I stood up I asked if I was allowed to present my side of the story. I was promptly told to keep my mouth shut.

The brave captain with his squad of marines said he didn't want any more firing up the beach. What an asshole. I'll call him "Dexter." As Dexter turned away to leave the gun position surrounded by his bodyguards, Moon said, "Shoot the asshole with the machine gun." I sure felt like it. You'll hear more about him in the future.

Anyway, the marines on the .50 calibers didn't fire down the beach anymore, so I guess we got our point across, even if they did get in the last word. I always thought I should have pressed charges against Dexter when I returned to the States after the war, but other things always seemed to be more pressing whenever the thought came to my mind. By now I understand what makes people like Dexter tick and believe they never advance past a certain basic stage of social and mental development.

We had four anti-aircraft batteries of three-inch guns on the island. In those days, the use of RADAR for detection of incoming flights was not available to "well-equipped" and "well-organized" outfits like the First Defense Battalion on Wake. But what few planes we had (Grumman F-2 or F-3 or maybe Brewsters) were pretty sharp as far as coordinating their efforts with the three-inch batteries. About two or three days before the Nips first hit us (December 8, 1941), the aircraft carrier *Enterprise* came within about 150 miles of Wake and launched twelve of the fighters which landed on our airstrip. I remember standing and watching them land. Five of the planes were destroyed on the ground during the first attack by the Japanese, and then we gradually lost the rest of them day by day.

I really thought the island command committed a gross error by not having all planes in the air after being warned by Pearl Harbor of the devastation the Nips inflicted on the Pearl Naval Base.

I remember the 22nd of December, watching a pilot coming in low over the water, right toward my gun position and he was obviously having problems with his plane. He turned right when over the beach above me and landed his plane on the beach wheels up.

You know, under normal circumstances here in the States, if you were to witness a plane in trouble landing you'd run over and try to get the guy out of the wreck. In this instance, the only thought which entered my head was either he was dead or he could get himself out of the mess he was in. This was "WAR" and it seemed in my own mind that all of us were expendable so why spend the effort. Any reader might think I was being inhumane by not trying to help, but the reader should not judge until he has the experience. I feel I was already adjusting my mental process to accept death when the inevitable came. Anyway, after a few minutes, the pilot jumped out of the plane, scratched his head and walked away into the bush to fight another day. I knew the pilot later on in China and learned to like him, even if he was a marine.

To get on with the story, one or two of our planes would go up daily to about 25,000 ft. and patrol around the island. Many times the pilots would spot the Nip bombers coming towards the island from miles away and would dive behind them to get on their tails like homing pigeons. Then the pilots would radio down to the AA batteries, giving the height, direction and speed which enabled the AA outfits to really take their toll. I am not sure, and neither is anyone else, how many bombers the AA put out of commission, but as I recall, they were credited with a couple dozen or so. I know they did a remarkable job, because in those days, before all the electronics, the AA batteries of any nation were not too effective. Also, the marines moved the AA positions every night so bombers wouldn't hit them the following day.

When the dive bombers came in on the island on the 21st, I learned how difficult it is to hit a fast-moving airplane with a machine gun. Each time a dive bomber came screaming in, I swore I was going to lead him enough so my tracers would enter the plane. We had every fifth shell a tracer. I knew shooting at a plane with a machine gun would be easier than shooting ducks on the Boise River in the 1930s. Anyway, I think about four or five dive bombers zipped past us and I didn't see any of my ammo going into the planes until the last one. I thought I had him dead to rights, but he just flew right on out to sea, just like some of the ducks I used to shoot and hit on the Snake River in Idaho. The last I saw of him, he was still going.

On the night of December 21, 1941, as we were sitting on the gun position, I was thinking what a wonderful episode this could have been in my life. The air here in the South Pacific was so balmy and soft it actually caressed your skin, and when the moon was shining, its beams of light made the ocean glitter with a million star flecks. No matter where you were on Wake Island, you could hear the gentle crash of the surf on the coral reefs and shore of the island. But then, there was a certain loneliness about Wake. It seemed the island had been waiting for thousands of years for someone to come along and speak to her and tell her how precious she was as part of God's beautiful world.

When I was growing up in Boise, Idaho, I had never dreamed anything like this little chunk of coral even existed. It was absolutely unbelievable these little men from the Land of the Rising Sun could turn my heaven, in which I had been so sublimely happy, into a hell in such a short time. And no matter how hard I might try to adjust and reroute my composure, I couldn't return to my yesterdays prior to December 8, 1941. Little did I realize on this night, there would be four years of hell before I would laugh again with the people I loved, in the land I loved so dearly.

The beautiful island which had been my Eden would now become my Hades.

In the long line of years which I was to traverse in my future earthly life, with all of the attending chances, I could never bring myself to return to this spit of coral, Wake Island, for even a flashback furnishes me with a melancholy reminder in which the past fades into history as the sunset dwindles into night.

CHAPTER 8

Taming the Warriors

On the night of December 22–23, 1941, the weather was cloudy and we would have a little rain squall every now and then. We were sitting on the gun position and listening to the surf and anything else we thought we heard. The surf, on a dark night, could sure fool a person into believing no matter what he was listening for, it would become a reality. You can actually talk to the ocean surf and it will answer you in the sweetest voice you have ever heard.

I had loaded the gun, as much as you can load a gun. About midnight or a little after, we began to see flashes of light on the horizon, intermittently. We thought this could mean several things were taking place. One, there was a battle going on between the Nip fleet and the U.S. fleet, for we knew the carrier *Enterprise* had been around this part of the South Pacific as little as four weeks ago. This was, of course, our fondest wish even though we knew in the depths of our hearts it wasn't so, or we would have heard at least some scuttlebutt on the battle. Two, the Nip fleet was clearing their guns in preparation for battle. Three, the Nip fleet ships were signaling each other with their search and signal lights. Actually, the most pragmatic application would be the last one, signaling.

I can remember how utterly depressed I was while watching those lights over the horizon. . . . I knew the war of my world was coming to a sudden climax and I was ill-prepared to face the enemy.

Our gun was about 50 yards from the surf and we had no sidearms. You can't use hand grenades in hand-to-hand combat. I knew one thing for certain, this little machine gun had better not fail me.

I walked over and talked to the first class bos'n, Binny, who was over in the bomb shelter, about the lights. I could tell by his face, none of his thoughts on the subject were encouraging.

I thought again how capricious life was for leading a 20-year-old boy from the little old Rocky Mountain state of Idaho along a path which would place him in jeopardy such as this. Moon and I hardly said a word to one another for the next eight or ten hours. I imagine his mind was filled with the same futile and disheartening thoughts as those racing through mine.

I had found a pair of leather work gloves to wear when firing the gun. Supposedly, the gun would get hot as the devil after firing continuously. Also, I had a screwdriver in my pocket to be used on a shell jam, even though the marines had warned me I would have to take the gun apart to remove a jammed round. What did those damn marines think they were going to be doing in the next few days, demonstrate Tupperware to the Nips? I had no idea on how to take it apart and even if I did I wasn't going to waste the time when a landing craft full of Nips was bearing down on me wanting to insert their bayonet into my rosebud.

I still get furious when I think of the damn marines putting us sailors down on the beach to take the brunt of the battle, and thereby committing certain suicide, when they were the ones who supposedly loved a good battle. If I had wanted to act stupid and macho, I would have joined the marines in the first place instead of taking this two-year naval detour. I was certain if anyone wanted a good battle, the little slant-eyed fellows who would be coming over the horizon pretty soon would give them one, especially when the odds were 500 to one.

Along about 0200 or 0300, even though still dark, we could see some of the ships coming over the horizon, and there were plenty of them. There were ships of all kinds, except we could see no aircraft carriers. We knew they would be laying farther off the island. It seemed we counted 30 or 40 of them and then quit counting. There were so many of them it was like counting chickens in a henhouse, you count the same chicken ten times and some not at all. As one last resort to bolster our faith in the U.S. Navy, I ran over to the bomb shelter and asked Binny if he recognized any of the silhouettes as being "our" ships. As usual when I wanted an answer all I had to do was look at his face. (Binny later died in prison camp from tuberculosis, I'm not sure where he was buried, somewhere in China. Another one "known but to God.")

You know, nowadays the United States is so damned involved with establishing everyone who died in Vietnam as accounted for or brought back to the U.S. for a hero's burial. We had thousands of men die in the South Pacific and China and we buried them wherever they happened to fall. I know very few of them were ever "relocated." So, as I say "known but to God."

Anyway, to get back to December 23, 1941, on the beach at Wake Island. A couple of hours before daylight, we saw two destroyers run up on the beach about one-half mile east of us. We didn't know it then, but a three-inch gun position was planted dead center right between the two destroyers, The Nips didn't know the gun was there or they wouldn't have chosen such a place to beach the ships. I thought the Japanese used beautiful military strategy in their battle plan. The airstrip was right there also. The Nips had planned on running landing craft in between the two beached ships and using the guns on the ships for protection against the defending forces. It seems the three-inch gun in this position was an anti-aircraft which didn't have a height finder so it couldn't be used against the bombers. Thus it was to be used against landing craft or bore-sighted against naval ships.

Most of the men manning the guns were part of the fighter squadron whose planes were destroyed or shot down at this point.

Anyway, they were bore sighting the three-inch and firing as fast as possible at the destroyers and landing craft. The firefight created a real, live, Fourth-of-July fireworks demo until the Nips finally overran the position and killed practically all of the crew. Of course, I learned most of the details after entering prison camp. It was really funny, after we became prisoners, we seldom said anything about the details of the battle. On this busy December morning, Moon and I didn't know how the battle was turning.

We started exerting extreme vigilance as far as surveying the surf in front of us. This was one time we wished we hadn't been invited to the party. It seemed to get darker as the dawn awakened. As I recall, the clouds moved in and covered the moon which had shone when we first had visions of the ships on the horizon. I don't know about Moon, but I was really uptight.

It must have been along about 0400 I heard something in the surf which sounded a little different than the norm. I asked Moon if he heard it and he said, "Yes." We concluded it sounded like an engine running, maybe a one- or two-cylinder diesel. Lo and behold, in a few more seconds, we could see the front end of a grey landing barge (boat). It was coming directly at us.

I told Moon I was not going to let it get to the beach before I opened fire because if we could get them running scared before they beached, they might back the barge down and leave us alone. So much for wishful thinking. I told him to get out some more belts of ammo as I turned the gun to fire on the barge and pulled the trigger.

What happened next is difficult to explain. As I have said before, it seemed I became mesmerized. I believe for a person to know what it's like to fire a machine gun at humans, the person would have to experience the action.

The old World War I water-cooled .30 cal. Browning kind of gave you the feeling you were operating a trip-hammer. It made a sound resembling a "slam-slam-slam" in your hand. I held onto the gun with both hands and used the tracers for sighting. I remembered the marine instructor saying you should fire the gun in bursts, but I wasn't very social with the Nips at the time and didn't care to get in any hand-to-hand combat. . . . If the "Sarge" wanted to fire the damn gun in bursts, I would gladly have traded him places.

We could see the barge fairly well from the light given off by the ricocheting slugs of the tracer ammo. I just kept firing while moving the stream of tracers like a water hose over the upper part of the barge.

The barge was built a lot like the design of our landing craft of later years in World War II. I can't remember ever seeing a landing craft in the United States Navy up to the time of the Pearl Harbor hostilities. We had a number of different designs of small boats but none of them resembled the later landing craft which were used in the South Pacific from '42 through '45.

Isn't it odd the United States Armed Forces didn't even anticipate the day sometime in the future when their armed forces may have to saunter up onto a beach in some far-off land?

The Nip barge had a ramp in the front and an armored housing around the pilot house to protect the bos'n while running the barge under fire. I could see the slugs were going right through the armor plating and if a .30 cal. would go through the armor, it certainly wasn't doing much in the way of protecting the men behind it. Also, I could see the slugs going through the bow of the barge.

We had a group of searchlights run by a batch of marines on the island. In the case of a landing by foreign troops at night, the search-lights were supposed to flip on and light up the landing area so the gunners of the different defense outfits could see what they were shooting at or to see what they should be shooting at and weren't. Well, you know how brave the marines were, letting a bunch of "swabbies" run their spearheads on the beaches for them.

Anyway, Moon and I yelled for the "searchlights" and someone must have heard us, and someone must have had a field phone because in a short time some searchlights shone down on the beach towards our barge target. As someone predicted, almost immediately, the lights drew fire from the enemy and the lights, without delay, were suffocated, never to shine again.

I wonder what brain in the Armed Forces thought up the idea of searchlights. They went out of vogue with the spear and arrow. I'm not even convinced they ever did any good shining on bombers so the anti-aircraft batteries could see what they were shooting, or trying to shoot, out of the sky.

The Ack-Ack at Wake Island found out the preferable way to ravage the enemy bombers was to establish the bombers' direction and height through intercourse with our fighters or initial use of height and directional finders and then set up a saturated window through which the bombers must fly. This method turned out to be very effective. Anyway, we had no help from the searchlights.

And now back to the beach. I kept firing a steady stream of slugs and Moon would have a new belt ready the instant I ran out of ammo. He and I were really a pretty good team. We liked each other, or rather I liked him very much and I always thought he liked me. He had tuberculosis in prison camp and I lost touch with him in 1943. I saw in a bulletin, published by the Wake Marines, that a "Moon" was living in Southern California but I don't know if it is him or not . . . hope so.

The belt of ammo on a Browning .30 caliber machine gun has a metal leader attached to the front of the belt. The ammo man can push the leader through the side of the breech opening and the gunner grabs the leader and pulls on it while working the breech. You can hear the lead round enter the firing chamber and lo, you are ready to fire.

Moon and I could hear voices coming out of the barge and once in a while a scream or yell. Then the most dreaded incident any machine gunner could experience, happened. We had a jam in the breech of the machine gun.

I thought I was going to freeze up, but much to my astonishment, I was really quite calm. Moon asked me what I was going to do now. I told him to grab a couple of the hand grenades and keep a watch on the beach in front of us.

Speaking of hand grenades, due to the fact we had stolen the grenades from the marines, we naturally hadn't received the United States Marine Corps two- or three-day field course in the nomenclature, etcetera, of the hand grenade and especially the art of throwing one of the little critters. I had heard talk around the island and seen movies in which the actors would lob the hand grenade in a wide arc with the arm extended to prevent the weight of the grenade from causing injury to your arm.

Also, I could remember "them" saying the grenade would explode in about eight seconds. Well, later in the battle, Moon and I threw several of the grenades, but we hauled off and threw them just like a green apple in a cow pasture. I couldn't worry about injury to my arm when my whole damn life and body were facing extinction.

You know, if the battle and my life were not so lamentable at this stage, it would have been very humorous. Not a darn thing was like "THEY" told me it would be. Everything was ass-backwards and upside-down. To think "THEY" told me on June 28, 1940, in Salt Lake City, where I was sworn into the United States Navy, if a war came I would be well-trained, clean, well-organized, well-fed, and well-paid. In essence, the only true statement "they" made on that day, so long ago, was "they" told me I would be in the Navy for six years and "they" were right on that score. Actually, "they" were even technically wrong on that score also, for I was attached to the Marine Corps for the next four years.

Now, back to the jammed machine gun. I had a screwdriver in my pocket and I flipped the breech of the gun open, reached down under the jammed cartridge with the screwdriver and flipped the shell out slick as a whistle. I closed the breech and pulled on the breech activator to load another shell and tripped the trigger and the gun commenced firing like God was running the show Himself. The "Man upstairs" was sitting right on my shoulder and don't you ever get the idea I wasn't conversing constantly with "Him," or rather I was talking and hoping "He" was listening.

After a period of time had passed, we had another problem with the gun. Because we were firing thousands of rounds through the gun, the barrel heated to the point where we ran out of cooling water. The Browning .30 caliber had a water jacket around the barrel to cool the gun. Well, Moon and I didn't have any water, and we sure as the devil weren't going down to the ocean right then to ask the Nips if we could have some. Moon knew where we could get some oil. I stopped firing and Moon took off to get the oil. He was only gone a few minutes, and during those minutes, no one came up the beach from the Nip barge. We filled the water jacket with the motor oil and left the cap off the filler opening so the jacket could breathe. The only problem with the oil was later on when we fired the gun for too long a duration, it would smoke like the devil, but at least we had our own smoke screen.

After we had completely riddled the barge and the people inside quit making any noises, we slacked off the continuous firing and started watching for any sign of life coming out of the barge.

All the time, it seemed there was a terrible battle going on up the beach between the two beached destroyers. We could see explosions aboard the destroyers and also an abundance of muzzle-blasting up on the beach. There was a navy twosome on a .30 caliber between us and the destroyers but we never did see them fire their gun. They must have been about 200 yards to the east of us.

At about 0500, it started to get light and was rather a cloudy day. Moon and I had fired about 8,000 rounds through the gun by this time, and we decided to try some hand grenades on the barge.

Moon took a couple of grenades and walked down about 100 feet toward the barge, pulled the pins and threw them. One of them went in the water and the second one went into the barge. I kept the gun ready in case any stranger showed himself as a threat to Moon.

Later on, I took a couple of grenades and threw them in the barge for some practice, or maybe because I was sure someone in the barge had a slug with my name on it.

Then we settled down to watching the armada of ships cruising on the horizon and closing on Wake. During this whole battle, Moon had been watching our backside, because we knew we couldn't depend on the marines.

While I was looking out to sea and watching the barge, I was wondering why the Nips had not tried to drop off the backside of the barge and go up or down the beach in the protection of the water. While I was watching for some movement, I saw a man coming out of the water. From where I was I could see he must have been gut shot. He crawled across the beach and dropped behind a fairly good sized boulder. While he was trying to make it from the water to the boulder, I didn't have the stomach to shoot him.

The only thoughts going through my mind was how I hated the bastards who inaugurated this fracas and how it was changing my life, and here I was having to decide whether I was going to be forced to kill a man I had never met and who probably had no axe to grind with me whatsoever, and probably had a family just like I did, and whose family presumably loved him the same as mine loved me. He was some mother's son whom she would never see until the "Man upstairs" decided whether they would meet again.

Moon and I talked about what to do. We knew if we took him prisoner, we ran the risk of being killed if he was booby-trapped. We had no sidearms with which to guard him. If he had a hidden sidearm, he could easily kill us both before I could cut him down with the machine gun.

After a short period of time, the man climbed up on a rock and sat down. He was close enough I could see he was sick. Probably from his wounds.

Then Moon and I decided he would have to be killed. I can remember right now as if it were yesterday, what a horrible gut wrenching pain I had when I finally made the decision. I asked Moon if he would shoot him and Moon said, "Hell, no, you're the gunner, you do it." I never did blame Moon for his attitude because if the positions had been reversed I would have responded likewise. The only solace we felt was, we considered every possible alternative that two young men who desperately wanted to live could envision at the time, under the circumstances. What would you have done under those conditions?

I put the gun on him and pulled the trigger. I saw the slugs tear into his torso, bouncing him off the boulder. I turned away and vomited. Why in the hell couldn't he have been a healthy Nip marine, charging me, with his bayonet fixed? In that event, I wouldn't have blinked twice at cutting him down. I still to this day dream about that man.

At about 0600, Moon said the asshole Marine Captain "Dexter" was headed our way with his bodyguard of marines following. Remember, this was the guy who had knocked me down a few nights previously, when I had returned some fire up the beach.

He came bouncing up to the gun position and said, "What is all this firing about down here?" What an asshole question, all he had to do was look at the barge in the surf and the answer should have been self-evident. And this was a "captain" in the Marines! He then said he would take care of the barge.

He and his marines marched down the beach to the barge and waded out into the water. There is an analogy of this action when General Douglas McArthur returned to the Philippines after the privates and grunts had killed or routed all the opposition.

Do you remember when he stepped out of a landing craft and waded triumphantly ashore with the background music playing "Stars and Stripes Forever"?

Then our brave captain said, with a hand grenade held high like the Statute of Liberty, "Surrender in the name of the United States of America," and then lobbed the grenade into the lifeless barge.

Do you know what I heard after the war was over? I have heard the Navy decorated him for subduing the Nip barge.

I can't believe people do the things they do. This is one of the foremost reasons I never go to the Wake Island Marines conventions held annually since World War II. I know if I ever see Dexter I would make a fool of myself, joyously.

Anyway, Dexter and his buddies went back up the beach and faded back into the bush from whence they came, and we didn't see them again until after we became guests of the Japanese Empire.

Soon after the encounter with Dexter, the Nips started sending in waves of dive bombers. Moon and I had decided we could stay on the gun position as sitting ducks on a snow-white beach, there was absolutely nothing around us but coral, or else we could retire the several hundred feet to the makeshift bomb shelter which was well-camouflaged with coral (the last time we used our gun against the dive bombers the .30 caliber was very ineffective to say the least). By this time of day, we could see out to sea very plainly and would have plenty of time to get to the gun if and when some landing party threatened our section of the perimeter.

All of the below quotation was copied from the book written by Commander Cunningham,[3] who was my commanding officer on Wake Island. My comments are in parentheses and italicized.

. . . Among the others bound for Wake was one of my (*Cunningham's*) shipmates in the *Wright* (*which was the ship that we took from Hawaii to Wake Island*), Commander Campbell Keene, a big, bald good-natured flyer who was leaving his assignment as head of the ship's air department to take a temporary command of his own on the island. Admiral Bellinger had made it clear to me (*Cunningham*) that we could expect frequent visits by patrol plane squadrons, one of which in fact was scheduled within a few days to cover the arrival of our own planes. Campbell Keene was to command a detachment that would help the flying boats in and out of Wake and control their activities while they were with us. It would be good to have him along.

With him for his mission he had thirty enlisted men and three ensigns, one of whom was a husky youngster name George "Bucky" Henshaw . . . . (*I was one of the thirty enlisted men mentioned above. I saw Commander Keene twice and some ensign three times in all our stay on the island. I mainly was in touch with a boatswain mate, who later died in China. I liked Binny. He was*

*kinda smartass before the shit hit the fan on December 8 but was
real down to earth after the first Nip took a shot at him. Binny was
in a lean-to on the beach with me on the last day before surrender
and later in the day after the landing barge encounter on the 23rd.)*

. . . . (*Cunningham goes on to say, regarding a battle*) It is worth
noting that communications almost never turn out to be fully
effective under the stress of battle. Conditions change with
lightning speed, mistaken observation results in faulty information, orders become inapplicable to the situation before
there is time to carry them out. Accounts of battles frequently
suggest that the commander has moved each of his formations
around like men on a chess board, but this is seldom the way it
happens. After the fighting begins, most decisions are made by
subordinate commanders on the spot.

For battles don't go according to plan. There is always confusion, whatever the advance preparation may have been. And
there was confusion in plenty on Wake.Little groups of defenders came under enemy attack and fought back without a chance
of coordinating their actions with any over-all plan. Both our
own troops and the Japanese were at times firing toward friends
as well as foes. From my command post, trying vainly to establish what was going on over the entire atoll, I could see tracer
bullets flying in all directions, and there is no doubt some of
the reports I had to assess were based on mistaken assumptions
as to who was firing the bullets. Further, the cut-off groups naturally tended to believe they were about the only ones left, and
what few reports we did get from them reflected such views.

. . . The invaders grounded two destroyer transports off the south shore of Wake and sent troops ashore from both. Two barges unloaded onto the beach at Wilkes. Two other landing craft put men ashore on Wake just east of the channel entrance. (*It was one of these two which Moon and I stopped with our gun.*) Other troops, as best can be determined, landed on Wake's inner shore from rubber boats that entered the shallow lagoon from the northwest.

As these landings began, the bulk of the active defense on Wake fell to mobile forces comprised of Marines, sailors and civilians, for a major portion of the defense battalion's strength was immobilized at the three-inch and five-inch guns. The area from Camp One eastward toward the airstrip was defended by . . . (*a lieutenant*) . . . and the defense battalion's mobile reserve, augmented by . . (*a boatswain's mate*) . . . and fifteen sailors (*the sailors were the only ones that really saw any action manning the three machine guns east of the channel and west of the airstrip, of which Moon and I manhandled the center gun position*) . . . and a considerable number of civilians. . .

. . . These were the hot spots on Wake as the fighting began. . . .

. . . At Camp One, landing craft approaching the channel were fired on by machine guns. . . .

. . . In his case (*Major Devereux*) of course, there was no necessity for me to recommend him for decoration, since both he and I were awarded Navy Crosses while we were prisoners.

I was, and remain, acutely aware that many deserving men went unrecognized in the distribution of honors. In the nature of things, medal-pinning is a hit and miss proposition. Many who receive them are less deserving than those who do not, and officers generally get a much higher proportion than they deserve. Behind many of the citations is an unwritten one that might go somewhat like this: "This medal was really earned by the enlisted men whose unrecognized devotion make him look good."

. . . To this day uncertainties remain as to who was killed on Wake and under what conditions. . . . [4]

We didn't know it at this time (around 0800 hours) but the Island Command had already surrendered the Islands. The Nips had broken through the line of defense which the marines had established up at the east end of the airstrip, which was opposite of the end where Moon and I were fighting. They had managed to land several thousand men and had the situation well in hand by the time they worked their way down to our end of the airstrip. They had captured the Command Post (CP) along with Major D.

About this time, a couple of sailors from the gun position east of ours came running down the beach and took over our gun position. I guess they figured we had deserted our post of duty, or thought they might get some kind of credit for stopping the barge. Anyway, Moon and I concluded the battle was about over and there was no way the United States was going to win this one.

As far as one could see in any direction, the Japanese navy had enough ships around Wake Island to enable a person to almost walk from ship to ship to the horizon.

You cannot conceive the blow to one's psyche which was going through each of us on that morning.

Around 1100 hours, we heard a voice over in back of the bomb shelter say we should lay down our arms and surrender. Then the voice identified itself as Major D, the commander of the marine garrison.

I had a couple of hand grenades on my belt, which I hurriedly buried in the coral. Then we crawled out of our dugout and held up our hands and surrendered to the several hundred Nip marines who were with the Major.

I am of the opinion I would never again surrender myself in such circumstances. It is so much easier to die than to endure the mental and physical punishment I experienced in the next four years.

CHAPTER 9

Taken

The Nips tied our hands with barbed wire and marched us back up the road to the airstrip. I was amazed, upon reaching the airstrip, to see the number of prisoners already sitting on the ground with their heads hanging like a bunch of beaten dogs. And my head was hanging too.

We hadn't eaten or had any water since yesterday. The Nips had machine guns all around the several hundred men sitting on the airstrip. I was certain they would, at some time in the near future, start killing us.

Sometime after 1300 hours, the Nips told us to take off all of our clothes, including our shoes. They wanted us stripped naked. Along about 1400 hours, they brought some 50-gallon drums on a truck with water in them. However, the drums had previously had gasoline in them, so the water was not drinkable. If you tried to drink the water, which I did, it burned your throat and mouth. We didn't have any water or food for the remainder of the day, nor the next day.

The Nip guards told us if we stood up we would be shot, immediately.

When the sun went down in the west and the night descended on the island, it turned cold. Remember we were naked. The Nips came around and gave us some rolls of tar paper to cover our naked bodies. Have you ever tried creating the latest Paris fashion with nothing but a roll of roofing tar paper? Not even thread and needle.

At about this time, the Nips took off our wire manacles. We dug holes in the airstrip and laid down a piece of tar paper. Then we pulled a piece of the tar paper over us. This was my first night as a prisoner of war of the Japanese Empire. They kept lights on us all night long.

The next day (December 24, 1941), the Nips didn't give us any water or food. We laid in our holes on the airstrip naked. On Christmas Eve, 1941, I remember lying in the hole on the airstrip and pondering over those wonderful Christmas Eves I had enjoyed as a child in the warmth of the home my loving parents had provided for me and which at the time, I really didn't appreciate to the extent I should have; but then, what young person does appreciate the love and consideration his family bestows on him? Would my Santa Claus ever come again?

On this night, and thousands of other nights in the years to come, I reminisced about my journey down through my life to the present point. I thought about all the different branches of my life's trail and tried to convince my God He should perform a miracle and posture me at any junction other than the one presently facing me. To no avail. At that moment on the airstrip, I think I was at the lowest ebb of my existence on this earth. But lo, the cascade of physical and mental agony was only in its initial stages.

This island and this war seemed to be occurring in an unfortunate dream in which the island no longer held any beauty nor did the sky, moon and ocean hold any connotation of romance or dreams of "what might have been." All of them emerged as evil challenges or obstacles to be surmounted in the face of this new, frightening despotism which seemed to permeate the very souls of the prisoners, of which I was one.

If one would want to see a metaphor of the spiritual dejection I saw in the other men's eyes, and thus their souls, one should view some of the pictures of the Jewish people of the holocaust of Germany during World War II. The same ghastly nothing was in their eyes. Would that I could see mine own in those terrible days and nights.

We received nothing to eat on Christmas Day 1941.

This was the first lesson to be learned provided you wished to subdue a population—starve them immediately until they become so weak there can be no physical resistance remaining in their bodies. At the same time threaten them with death by giving them stringent guidelines of activities which no average person can possibly obey. Watch intently for any violation of the above guidelines and impose the death penalty immediately.

I was to learn many things from my little yellow captors from the Land of the Rising Sun.

On the third day of capture (December 26), the Nips moved us up to Camp Two, where they had built a holding compound out of posts and wire. We were also given clothes to wear (a pair of pants, shirt, and shoes, if you could find a pair to fit).

As soon as we were captured, the officers were separated from the enlisted men and were never allowed to mix after that time. It was one of the Nips' strategies to always keep the officers separate, their thinking being the enlisted men were very mediocre in comparison to the officers, and without direction could not conceive or plan any escape or other disrupting activity.

In the Nip armed forces, the officers can, without any significant excuse, kill their subordinates at will.

The officers were held in high esteem by the Nips. They were not permitted to work. They received all the food their hearts desired. Their food was substantially of better quality. As far as we knew, the officers never were beaten or abused, as were the enlisted men. They received pay from the Japanese, at the Japanese officers' pay scale, all the time they were interned. They were allowed to purchase goods from the Japanese Commissary (so to speak) at times. They were given a number of enlisted personnel to serve as butlers or "tobans." In other words "to wait on them as stewards." They always had their clothing and uniforms, including shoes, the same as if they were still in the States.

During the stay as a guest of the Japanese, I came to dislike the class discrimination between the officers and enlisted men, immensely. I can remember being hungry as hell and having one of the officers pass me on the way to the "john" and wanting to paste him in the face. You know, in a period of years, a degrading situation such as this can really change your conviction as to the meaning of the Bill of Rights and the Constitution of the United States.

United States Armed Forces are great for the underground source of information and communications systems. The service men call this method of communicating scuttlebutt, or at least this is what it was called when I was in the service. Maybe it is known as something else in this "modern" day and age of "Newspeak." Well, as soon as we were ensconced in the luxury of the Nipponese POW holding pen on Wake, the scuttlebutt started to fly, everything from having the U.S. Navy just over the horizon to repatriation of everyone within 48 hours. Of course, none of it was ever to come true. In the later years, though, in the prison camps to come, some of the scuttlebutt would turn out to be surprisingly accurate.

Along about the 12th of January, 1942, we were told most of us would be put on a ship and sent to Japan. The shipboard commandments were comparable to the Lord's when He was talking to Moses by the burning bush. Below is a sample.

The prisoners disobeying the following orders will immediately be put to death:

> …Those talking without permission and raising loud voices…

> …Those touching the boat…

> …Those carrying unnecessary baggage while embarking…

> …Those taking more meal than given them……. etc…

I never did understand why, but in at least a half-dozen instances, the Nips took all of the enlisted men's clothing away from them but allowed the civilians and officers to keep their clothing. Also, when we were put aboard the prison ship to Japan, we were told if we tried to take any clothing, other than what we were wearing, we would be put to death. Which, incidentally, scared the shit out of me, and so I did as I was told. The officers took all of their clothing (both cold weather and summer dress, including numerous pairs of shoes) along with them, enough to fill a footlocker. The same with the civilians, who took everything but the kitchen sink with them.

Both of those groups were also allowed to keep their money they had on them when the war started. I remember one marine sergeant named "Hardway," who had a diamond ring and stuffed it up his rectum to bootleg it past the Nips.

While we are on the subject of Hardway, I might as well tell how some days things will never go well for a person no matter how hard one tries. Hardway was an older marine, I would guess to be about 35 years at the beginning of World War II. Before he left the States in 1941 to join up with the First Defense Battalion (which ended up on Wake), Hardway was married to a gal who really wasn't the kind of girl who married "dear old dad." Just a few days before he was to board ship for Pearl (remember, in those days you didn't run out and jump on a jumbo jet to Hawaii), he went home for lunch unexpectedly, and found his wife in bed with another marine, but before he could divorce her or cancel his insurance naming her beneficiary, or his pay-allotment to her, he was on the ship headed for Wake Island. And before he could get any communication to the mainland from Wake, the war started and thus, he could never negate all the niceties a loving husband gives to a loving and trustworthy wife. Then, for the crowning blow which is certainly a mockery of justice, Hardway died in 1944 in Woosung Prison Camp of tuberculosis. Thus his wife even got his government life insurance and everything the man had in the world. The irony of life!

Anyhow, the evening came when we were to load on the *Nitta Maru*, which was to be our home on the briny deep for the next week or ten days. I never could compute how many days we were on the tub. I remember it was a stormy day and dark, with a rain squall coming up every now and then. It made the metal decks slippery as hell.

We were all loaded on barges and taken out alongside the *Nitta Maru*. We were told to jump from the barge to the ladder which went up to a hatchway in the side of the ship, about 60 or 70 feet up from the edge of the barge. Because the ocean was so rough, the barge would bang the side of the ship and then swing away from the ship about ten feet. If you missed the ladder when you jumped, you would fall down between the barge and side of the ship and be crushed to death. We lost some men in loading, but I don't know how many. The Nips didn't care whether you made the "one great leap for mankind" or not. They made no effort to make sure you got aboard the *Nitta Maru* safely. If a situation like that occurred today, someone would be greeted with one whale of a liability suit. I still can't get over the astronauts' families being paid millions, just because the Columbia space ship destructed. Hell, we lost ships at sea in WW II with 5000 men on board and their families got zilch. I think it's a bunch of horse puck the way we baby the citizenry. And then the young people whine about paying social security taxes when they haven't earned the right to be a citizen in any sense of the word, as yet. Let them give five or six years of their lives, for no pay, to the service of the country and maybe risk their lives and then maybe, just maybe, they should be allowed to be a citizen.

Anyway, back to war, when it came to be my turn to jump for the ladder, I said a little prayer or maybe it was a big prayer, and jumped, and made it. You couldn't pry my hands off the ladder with a stick of dynamite, after I once snared the thing.

As I went through the hatchway a couple of Nips hit me with clubs and I ran down a passageway (sort of a guided tour sponsored by the Nipponese) to the entrance of the hold hatchway, and down the ladder I went into the bowels of the ship, which smelled like death. And turned out to be a fiendish death for three of my friends.

Of the several hundred civilians who were left on the island, all but 100 were later sent by ship to Japan. Then in 1943, the remaining prisoners on Wake Island were lined up in front of a common grave and machine-gunned to death. I imagine this is one way to solve problems. What a magnificent civilization we live in today.

Really, how much progress has been achieved in the last four thousand years?

If you've never been down in the hold of a ship, it's quite an intimidating experience. They carry all of the cargo in the hold of the ship provided they want it out of the weather and stowed in a fairly secured position when encountering foul weather at sea.

Weather at sea can be tremendously dominating with the ground swells which can be 40 or 50 feet high and they can hide a good-sized ship from view provided the ship is in the trough of the swell.

Swells usually occur when the ocean is under stormy conditions, in which the water is pitching, blowing and wavy. The waves can be high enough to come over the flight deck of an aircraft carrier, some 30 to 50 feet high . . . and if the ship is headed into the wind and under way at ten to twenty knots, the flight deck will really take a bath. Add to this the pitch and roll (sometimes 30 degrees) and you'll really believe the Lord can generate energy... even enough to create a cleavage in the Red Sea.

Now, back to the hold of a ship. The ship is made so the hold goes from the weather deck down to the hull of the ship. Actually, the hull is covered with what is termed a double bottom to give the ship a flat deck at the very bottom instead of being a "V" shape.

The hull really looks like a "V" if you could see it cross sectioned from the bow or the stern. Then this hold may be divided into a number of decks or floors, so to speak. The hold will have a hatch port, or door, on the side of the hold by which persons can enter the hold and climb down a ladder. The top of the hold is usually covered after the cargo is loaded and battened down or secured.

Into such a hold is where we were to spend the next ten days or two weeks on the high seas, with the top hatches battened down securely, with no way out in case the ship sinks. This actually was the case in a number of Nip prisoner-of-war ships during the transporting of POWs from the Philippines and Asia proper.

We climbed down the ladder and were crowded up together like sardines. The Nips had a couple of smaller lights which dimly lit the hold. In each of the four corners of the hold, they placed a five-gallon can for us to use for "benjo" . . . which is going to the john or can. I guess this was the origin of the jargon "can" . . . get it? "John" or "Can."

We were again warned we would be shot immediately if we violated any act contrary to strict shipboard discipline, and I mean the Japanese have discipline in their lives, quite different from the discipline practiced in the United States.

They had a machine gun at the only passageway door leading from the hold. We were told to lay down at all times except when permission was given to go to benjo. We were fed once a day with a cup of rice gruel which smelled and tasted like raw fish. You can imagine what the place smelled like . . . almost everyone had dysentery. The benjo cans were always occupied, so the spillover and the vomit which men couldn't control, went on the deck.

We were laying in this filth, with the ship pitching in the storms and with the attitude of "what-the-hell-difference-does-it-make-anyway" to men who believed they were at the tail end of their lives.

We felt for sure within the next few days, we would either be shot, torpedoed by one of our submarines, or die from our retching and vomiting. Talk about a miserable bunch, it was terrible. There were about 1,000 of us in the hold, both civilians and servicemen.

For some reason, only God knows, about the time we went aboard ship, my dysentery stopped, and I didn't see it again until we were well into the sedate prison camp life. Added to the good fortune, which didn't really impress me at the time, I was never seasick. I believe this discipline was the one and only good endowment which came out of my engine room training aboard the *Tangier* in my early navy days.

About the second or third day at sea, we heard the call for battle stations and the siren which meant the ship or the escort ships had sighted a submarine. The weather was already about as rough as it could possibly get. Each time the bow climbed a wave, I thought the *Nitta Maru* would destruct from the force of the storm.

There was tons of activity aboard the ship, with Nips running everywhere and screaming different commands. I was hoping the guard didn't get nervous and start shooting. I can't believe how many times I said my prayers during the trip. I'm sure I learned all there is to know about stress in the time spent aboard the *Nitta Maru* on the ocean cruise.

I remember thinking over and over in my mind exactly what my options were if a torpedo hit the side of the ship. One, I knew the Nips would not uncover the hatch on the hold so we possibly could swim out of this cesspool. Two, I knew I would be unable to swim out the same hole the torpedo blasted in the hull because I was not a strong swimmer. I often thought of the instructor in boot camp saying, "If you can swim 60 yards, you will be able to get away from the ship as it goes down." Little did he know that not only would I have to get away from the ship, but also get out of this damned hold first.

Thus, it seemed my only likelihood of survival in the event the U.S. submarine hit us with a "fish," was the torpedo would only cripple the ship and allow the *Nitta Maru* to stay afloat.

Every time the ship would slam a swell in the storm, we knew a torpedo had hit some other part of the ship. There weren't any of us who had ever been in a naval battle and experienced a torpedo explosion on the ship.

While on Wake, we knew a friendly submarine was in the area, for it was credited with sinking a Japanese cruiser or destroyer. And we were confident it was this sub which was now following us.

Anyhow, the submarine didn't attack us, so maybe he got a shot at one of the escorts.

WHY THEM?

When the Lord calls men to heaven's doors

Are they called to Him when ready to go?

Or is it some other factor He knows

Which tells Him they're ready to grow.

— dkk

At this same time, maybe before the sub alert or after, a couple of Nip naval officers came down in the hold, with an interpreter. They wanted to know if there were any U.S. Navy men who had been trained in the Navy Air arm of our armed forces. Well, after volunteering for Wake Island, you couldn't get me to volunteer for a free night in paradise with the best babe Hollywood had to offer. Anyway, three men I knew around the island stood up. I'll call them Chunky, Mex and Hotdog.

I remember Chunky was a nice, young, fat and happy Mormon boy from Ogden, Utah. I liked him very much. He was one of the three Naval Air type sailors who was lying right next to me during the voyage so far.

The Mex was the other man I knew fairly well. He was braver than almost any man I had ever met. He was always charging around on Wake with a different gun (where he managed to acquire them, I don't know). Every time I would see him, he would be looking to see if the Nips had arrived. He was only about five feet tall, but boy, what guts!

Hotdog was a sailor who I had seen around Wake Island but didn't know too well.

All three of them were laying close to me when they volunteered to go topside with the Nip interpreter. This was the last moment in this life I was to see these men.

We didn't know it then but the Nips took the three of them up topside (weather deck), and made them kneel down and tied their hands behind them. Then the Nips had a big crowd gather around to exalt the superiority of the Nip navy evidenced by the conquering of Wake Island (big deal). One of the officers then took his samurai sword and hacked the heads off of all three of the men.

The heads of the men didn't come loose from their necks on the first whack, and the Nips had to hack and hack until they were finally beheaded. In the postwar crime trials, some of the Nips at the beheading ceremony said even the witnesses were sick at their stomachs from viewing the gruesome atrocity.

The Nips then took the three bodies and heads and dumped them overboard. All three of these men should have been awarded the Navy Cross.

In 1945, when I returned home, I was at my folks' house when we heard a knock at the door one afternoon and an older couple, about 45 or 50 years, was there and wished to talk to me. They introduced themselves as the father and mother of the beheaded sailor "Chunky," who I knew on Wake.

They had ridden the train all the way from Ogden just to talk to me. I don't know why but the U.S. government didn't have information diddly-squat about prisoners lost or missing in the Orient. These poor people had not heard a word about their boy even in November 1945. I told them what I could about their son and what I had heard about the executions. I felt so sorry for them. I still have a tremendous hatred for causes which initiate such sadness and pain.

We were on the ship ten or so days. I lost track of time. I could tell I was getting weaker by the minute and my zest for living was diminishing rapidly. All the lying around with about 300 calories a day in the form of the rice gruel for body nourishment and breathing the foul air with the smell of puke, shit and death kept your gut wrenching 24 hours a day.

At last I heard the turbines begin to slack off, which told me we were either in an emergency, like a torpedo attack, or we were coming into port.

During the last few days, I didn't seem to care whether I lived or died, but with the hope the prison ship had made the islands of Japan or the China continent, there seemed to be a new small fiber of life sparking somewhere down in the depths of my soul and body. You know, it's difficult to tell where your body ends and your soul begins, they both seem to fade into one another.

There were several of the prison ships, coming up from Singapore, Hong Kong and the Philippines, with thousands of prisoners on board. A number of them were attacked by submarines and sunk, with all those men going down to a watery grave in the bowels of those ships. Why don't we insist a huge war memorial be built to honor them specifically or give them some type of special recognition for the hell they went through in their dying gasps as their life was smothered by the ever increasing darkness in the watery depths? It takes very little intestinal fortitude to win a medal of honor compared to slowly dying in the hold of a prison ship which has a 20-foot hole in its ribs. Every one of those men who died should be awarded our country's highest honorable medal.

Soon after the engines slowed, they were shut down and I could feel the ship being tied up to some pier or similar docking structure. Not much occurred for the next day or so. Then I could tell the ship was under way and heard the engines start again. I thought "aw shit," the Nips probably missed and hit Africa or some damn place which would cause us to be out on the ocean again, exposed to more submarines.

What really happened was the Nip army in charge of prisoners was not organized to handle any bodies as yet. Therefore, they decided to take us to China.

China, for all intents and purposes, was entirely dominated and controlled by the Japanese in January 1942.

We had to cross the China Sea and go into the Yangtze River in the vicinity of Shanghai, China. The trip took about five days. We tied up in the evening of a day when it was raining and windy. When I finally got to see the outside world, I thought how much it reminded me of the scenes depicted by Edgar Allen Poe in the "Raven". . . the night when wicked atrocities happen to unsuspecting souls.

About an hour after tie-down, the Nips told us to climb out of the hold and gave us another club-guided tour of the ship. They ran us down a gangplank and lined us up on a dock. I remember the horrible smell which is constantly associated with China and their different customs, one of which is to collect their bodily solids and carry them to their fields to be used for fertilizer on the crops. As far as you could see the land was flat. I still don't know how or why the Nips or Chinese built the dock clear out in the middle of no-where. The thought crossed my mind, continuously, that this may be where they were going to massacre us because of the number of machine guns positioned around the area.

CHAPTER 10

Killing of Souls

Finally, after all of the prisoners were out of the prison ship, the *Nitta Maru*, a dignitary of some type stood on a truck or some piece of equipment and gave us a speech. He told us they would try not to kill all of us. If we did as we were told and helped them build a Co-Prosperity Sphere of Greater-East Asia, one day we would maybe return to our defeated homeland.

We were all very weak from the trip in the hold of the ship and the environment which went with it. I had on a pair of khaki pants and a khaki shirt. Also, I had on a pair of Marine Corps shoes which fit me fairly well. But as I stood, at attention, in the drizzle, I was getting colder and colder. After the character finished his pep talk, a contingent of Nip army soldiers marched up and lined us out for a march, destination unknown. There were about a thousand of us, civilians and servicemen.

At this point in time, we were all from Wake Island; whereas, later on in the prison days, we had prisoners with us from all over Asia. Actually, eventually, we were so diluted it became a matter of great concentration to even remember where the guy working next to you was captured.

As we started marching down a narrow road, three or four abreast, it gradually grew darker and darker. In China the roads are mainly cart tracks of dirt. Once in a while a road will be made of cobble stone or brick. Many of the roads I worked on when a prisoner, were made of bricks.

I talk to many of the modern day American tourists, who try to tell me China has changed completely since I was there and the only retort I have is, they've not really seen China. They go on one of the guided tours and think they are qualified to expound on the innermost facets of life in China. To discern the life of the Chinese, one must migrate to the backcountry and live among the people. The Chinese in and around the tourist traps are not symbolic of the masses.

After a while the rain stopped and we still walked, and walked, and walked. I'm not sure how far we walked but it must have been eight or ten miles until we could see in the distance some buildings which looked similar to the old hog hutches we used to use on the farm in Ola, Idaho, where I worked in the summer of 1939. They were somewhat larger to accommodate the size of man.

Finally we walked into the compound which was to be our home for the next year. The Woosung Forts.

The Forts were originally built by the Chinese back prior to 1930, and were situated in the delta of the Yangtze River not too far from Shanghai. There was a great battle around the Forts in 1937, when the Japanese invaded most of China and Manchuria.

Page Three

Prisoner

DARE KEENE KIBBLE

Mr. and Mrs. Marion Calvin Kibble, 1209 North Twenty-second street, received word Tuesday afternoon their son, Dare Kean Kibble, fireman second class, U. S. Navy, is a Japanese prisoner. The letter from the Navy department said a Red Cross delegate in Tokio reported him held by the Japanese as a prisoner of war, but place of his confinement was not disclosed.

It was the first word Mr. and Mrs. Kibble had about their son in nearly six months. He was a graduate of Boise high school, and enlisted in the Navy two years ago at the age of 18. Last year he completed a fireman's training school at Norfolk, Va., and had been recommended for promotion to first class just before the engagement in which he was captured. Details were not revealed.

Boise local newspaper article reporting Dare Keane Kibble's POW status.

China has a most bizarre impact on a person when you are out amongst the people, especially in the farming country. . . . Every component of life is so contrary to Western civilization, provided you can call the society in which we live today civilized, you tend to become mesmerized by the extreme variance in living methods and habits. I can see how the Chinese people can totally absorb a whole culture as if they never were.

We were in no certain order when we were marched into the compound, military and civilian were mixed. They called for all civilians to form in one group, three or four deep, and the same with the servicemen. Then the Nips told us to further group into sectors of 32. The Nips then told the officers to appoint the ranking non-coms, one to each sector, to be in charge of the section, so to speak. I was to be in Section Four, Barracks Two. Then we were told to count off starting with number one. I was number seven (shitshi). Later upon leaving China I was assigned the number two hundred fifty three (ni-hyaku-goju-san). It is amazing today (1990) how many times in the last 40 years, I have opened a book, looked at a clock, or being a CPA doing audits, run across that number with all the reversionary flashbacks.

The officers were quartered in their own section of our barracks and were entirely separated from us. We were not allowed to go near their end of the barracks at any time.

When I speak of "barracks," I don't mean to insinuate our barracks were a facsimile or in any way similar to the barracks furnished the U.S. servicemen. There were six sections to the barrack building and in each section there were four built-up wooden platforms. Eight men slept on each of the four platforms. There was a hallway which ran down the full length of the building. Half of a section bay was on each side of the hallway. Sixteen men were in each half of the bay.

The floors were made of single one by six lumber and you could see through the knotholes to the ground. The mice and rats loved these escape hatches. There was one light in each half-bay. There was no water in the buildings nor was there any heat whatsoever anywhere in the camp, except the cook shack. The benjos (toilets) were out in back of the barracks and included about ten stalls with slit floors. Under each slit in the floor was an earthen crock which held about 30 gallons of "farm juice" (or "elixir of life"), which was dipped out periodically and applied to the adjacent farmer's fields. Sometimes you were furnished with a type of brittle straw-paper to wipe your south end with and if not, you wiped with the finger and rinsed the finger at an outdoor water hydrant. And if you were sick enough you didn't give a damn whether you wiped or not. There was always a sufficient supply of flies and mosquitos.

Our section was assigned a section leader whom I will call "Brownnose." He was a southerner from Louisiana, I believe.

We were then told to go into our barracks and sections. Around this time, we were told to take off our clothes and they issued us a pair of Nip army pants, shirt and shoes, none of which fit. The pants and shirt would fit a twelve year old boy and the shoes were about size tens whereas I wear size eights. Everything was second-hand, nothing in Japan seemed to ever be new.

In our section, I was quartered with Brownnose, Louie, Red, Jackie, Dutch, Oldman and Hardway. I was to sleep, eat, shit, work, fight, freeze and pray with these guys 24 hours a day for two years until I left China for Japan in 1943. In those days I would get so sick and tired of their faces and problems, I thought I would go insane. Louie was the only one I could really talk to.

Brownnose seemed like a man who probably joined the Marine Corps to live the life of luxury, coming from Louisiana. Incessantly he would talk about black-eyed peas and sow belly. He never had married and was about 35 years old with about fifteen to sixteen years in the Corps. When you heard him talk about a woman, you could understand why no woman would marry him. If an officer told him to eat dog dung, he would say, "How much, Sir?" He must have been up brown-nosing with the officers in our barracks because he still wore Marine Corps clothing of a sorts. And he always seemed to be able to get next to a razor, for he always wore a well-cropped mustache. Brownnose was always scared to death one of us in his section was going to escape. The Nips told everyone if anyone escaped, the section leader would be shot immediately and then later on, the rest of the section would be shot. Every once in a while, we'd give ol' Brownnose a scare by telling him if he didn't mind his "Ps" and "Qs" we would go over the hill. I never saw Brownnose after I left the China camps in 1943. In later years, I heard he had retired from the Corps and gone back down South to live.

Hardway was really a dichotomy for I could never envision him as a marine. Hardway never spoke of his mother or father. He seemed to be exceptionally well-read and may even have had a couple of years of college. He had large feet and hands which would lead one to believe when in "natural" life, he would weigh around 200 pounds. He was about six feet tall and had rotten teeth. He is the person I referred to who hid a precious stone from the Nips by stuffing it up his rectum.

I used to love to listen to some of Hardway's escapades during his previous life, prior to enlisting in the Corps. I remember one such venture so well. He had hitched rides by rail and road to Southern California with a friend during the late thirties (1937–38–39). When they couldn't get jobs anywhere they decided they had to do something before they starved to death. So they decided to collect donations for various philanthropic organizations such as the Red Cross and March of Dimes. Well, it seems as how going from door to door, they not only were given extensive amounts of money which they pocketed but many ladies fed them and bedded them. I guess they lived in this fashion for a year or so until their conscience did 'em in. Right after this escapade they decided to join the Corps. Hardway was the one who was scalped by his wife as was mentioned earlier in this epistle. I thought as much or more of Hardway than I did of any other marine I have known. He was intellectual to the point you would never know he was a typical overbearing marine unless he wanted to reveal such. Hardway stayed in China when I left in 1943. He died in China of tuberculosis in 1944 and as far as I know is buried near the camp called "Kiangwan." The spelling of the camp name may be in error but the phonetics are close.

Louie was my buddy all the time I was in China (1942-43). He was a marine and hated the Corps like you can't believe. He was about my size and build. He was very adamant about putting every impediment in the Nip Co-Prosperity Sphere program you could possibly imagine. Normally, when the section was sent on a work detail, the total section would be given a quota of work to accomplish or no-eat. Louie would always lay back and push the Nips as far as possible, thereby getting the whole section in trouble. The rest of the section was continually giving Louie hell for not carrying his share of the load and many times I would side with Louie because I thought he was right. So sometimes I would catch hell also. Many of the guys would try to talk me into ignoring Louie when he would try his sit-down working habits. I was the only sailor in several sections of our barracks, but the marines in my section, after six or eight months had passed and I had a couple of fights with marines, said I wasn't half-bad for a sailor. This acacknowledgment was analogous to a medal of honor coming from any marine. They said I was a good worker provided I didn't side with Louie. Louie was from St. Louis, Missouri. I gathered his parents had difficulties in his early life for he never talked much about them. In fact, as I ponder now, it seems most of the men I knew during the war, in the Marines, came from broken homes. There was little love girding their lives during their childhood.

A very unique idiosyncrasy occurred in the prison life, in most every case, almost without exception. When the men were assigned to groups or sections, they would always pair off. Always seeking someone to cleave to as if some supernatural force demanded the individual recognized he was not sufficient unto himself. For instance, in our quarter-bay, the pairs were Brownnose-Oldman, Hardway-Dutch, Jackie-Red, Louie-Kibble. You might present the question, "but if you divide eight by two, they must break off in pairs." Not so, for I have seen odd-numbered groups break off in pairs leaving a single. And in each case, the single would eventually get sick and either die or seek out and affiliate with another single. Threesomes never occurred except occasionally; and then, only momentarily. Nor do I remember a foursome ever.

I'LL SEND YOU A HELPER

Lord, I know you promised to send

A strong hand in the day of my strife.

A helper someday You would lend

For me to navigate life.

But Lord if a helper you give me

Please let me look in his eyes,

And through some undefinable power to see

And my helper to recognize.

— dkk

At all times, Louie and I would take care of each other's interests and actually feel genuine compassion for each other. Without any conversation between us, we would always interface so as to act as one body regarding our mutual interest. This had nothing to do with sex but seemed to be a matter of life or death.

Our loyalties seemed to be responsive by groups, with the pairing of individuals being of foremost importance and thus on up the ladder. The complete groupings were: 1. as Americans. . . 2. as servicemen. . . 3. as sections. . . 4. as quarter-bays. . . 5. as pairs.

I could never completely comprehend the pairing force, but I feel now it stems from the indestructible desire God generates in man to seek fellowship, whether it be man, or woman, or beast.

Anyway, Louie and I became very close and I felt a twinge of loneliness when I was separated from him in 1943.

Dutch was the typical marine. I believe he was of German descent, fair complexion, square build, powerful in the body, military bearing, loved the Corps. He had found a home and would stay as long as allowed. He was friendly with me to a degree, but always remembered I was navy. Probably one of the most disciplined men I ever knew. I heard later he stayed in the Marine Corps for thirty years and retired to I know not where.

Oldman was an older man, I'd say about 45 years old. He was a Norwegian. Oldman had not been in the Corps too long and I'm not sure how he got in at his age, but I think he had been in the Army for a number of years and somehow transferred over to the Corps. He had one of those complexions which made him look as if you could scrape the dirt or grime from his body. He was about the most beat-up character I have ever seen. He reminded me of an old north woods logger. I liked him and he was always friendly with me. Good ol' boy.

Jackie was a reserve marine who had been called into active duty and wasn't the brightest boy around. In fact, most of the marines who I knew weren't all so very bright. I honestly believe if you want to be a marine, you were dealt a short deck in the second story. If you asked Jackie a question, you needed abundant time on your hands to secure the answer, provided one was coming. I never did hear what happened to Jackie after 1943. Maybe he didn't make it back. He and Red were a perfect pair. Red was even younger than I was (20). He came in the Corps under the "get out at 21" program. He was red-headed, pigeon-toed and kind of walked like he had a screw loose somewhere. He was a very sincere, nice guy. I see by reading the tabloid, *Wig-Wag*, I receive periodically from the Wake Marines organization, Red is still kicking around and enjoying life with his wife.

You know, being a sailor on Wake presented many a dilemma, but one primarily which pestered me over the last 45 years, is the lack of brotherhood between Armed Forces units. I have never felt like I was a member of any unit. I left the Army Field Artillery in the National Guard and joined the Navy. When the war started I was fighting with the marines and they never really accepted me. So out of six years of being in the service, I could never really claim any branch as my home. I tried to go to a USS *Tangier* reunion in the summer of 1988, but I only knew three men out of the whole ship's company and I had left the *Tangier* before hostilities occurred, so we had very little in common for conversation.

In the winter of 1942, we were a miserable gang of prisoners. For the months of January through April, it was cold and, at times, snowy. The Nips allowed us to stay in the barracks for those first few months. We stayed in bed to keep warm. Have you ever tried to stay in bed 24 hours a day? We had two blankets each. If you lost a blanket you would be shot immediately, without trial. The blankets were made of wool and when you tried to fold them down around you, they would stick straight out like a starched apron.

To correct this quirk in the blanket industry's quality control, we would, all eight of us, sleep together. In this way, we had sixteen blankets and the sheer weight of the wool tended to curl the edges of the blankets.

We would take turns as to who would be *numero uno* and *numero ocho*. The outside sleepers were much more frigid than the insiders. We would sleep, at all times, on our sides. After so long on one side, someone would say "SHIFT" and everyone would switch sides. You either cooperated or got some fists in the ribs. It didn't take long to get everyone's collaboration. If you lay on your side for three or four months on a wooden bed, you get vicious, infected sores on your hips and legs. Also, your skin begins to resemble fish scales. So don't "pooh-pooh" the next time someone hints you may have come from the "Great Waters." Remember, we did not wash, change or remove clothes, bathe, brush teeth, comb hair, or shave, in those four months. We relegated our activity to three movements: eating, potty, and sleeping.

Our food the first night we arrived in the forts was a thick, curried gravy with meat and vegetables, a large cup of it. We thought maybe the life in China wasn't going to be too bad. But after the first meal, the dietician must have died or was fired because this meal was the last good meal for the next four years. The standard meal, usually three times a day, was a small teacup of boiled barley, sprinkled generously with rocks and nails. Much of the grain we received in China came from empty boxcars. The Nips would come into the prison and grab a work detail of eight or ten men, who were taken by truck to the railroad yards outside of Shanghai, and there they would sweep the dregs from the floors of the barley cars.

Thus we would receive the foreign elements, such as rocks and nails, which sifted to the bottom of the cars in transport. When our cooks would wash the barley, the dirt would float out, but not the heavier elements.

Also, once a day, we would get a daikon soup. A soup wherein you put one daikon (daikons are similar to large winter white radishes), a dash of soy sauce and gallons of water. You would get a small teacup of the soup.

We estimated we were receiving about 800-1000 calories per day. We started to lose weight rapidly. Most of the men, including me, went down to around 105-115 pounds, and sustained such weight for the next four years.

The methods used in the prison to control social and economic injustices were quite unique and very practical. If only the greater society would use similar methods.

For proper distribution of food and to make certain no one received more than their portion of food, the following system was devised and strictly enforced and I mean strictly. A wooden bucket with a food ration for sixteen men was distributed twice a day. Each bay contained sixteen men, and would elect by voice vote initially, the man who would serve for a couple of weeks as "toban," or food server. After the initial selection, the privilege would rotate around the bay. However, if a person did not want to exercise his right then it could be passed to his appointee.

The toban would set up sixteen metal bowls and disperse the gummy barley with a facsimile of a ping-pong paddle. The bowls belonged to each individual, with some being clean and some being grimy. You also had a spoon with which to eat. The bowl resembled a cup from which to drink hot water or the watery daikon soup. After the toban dispersed the barley, if there was any complaint, a person could speak up and any unequal food distribution would be rectified. Every person, at any time, could elect to substitute his portion for any other person's ration with no questions asked.

We had some fisticuffs at the beginning until the system wore in and then everyone settled down. With 32 pairs of hungry eyes watching every morsel, the toban readily became an expert at distributing equal rations, even to the grain.

It was mutually agreed, if any individual decided to go over the hill, he would tell the section of his plan so we could all go over the hill at the same time. The Nips simply and emphatically stated, when anyone tried escape, all in the section would be shot immediately. And to enforce their determination, they shot the first escapee.

The Japanese were masters at establishing discipline in individuals, crowds or nations. In 1942, the population in the city of Shanghai determined they would have a mass rally in one of the large squares in the city. The Japanese told the Chinese ringleaders this type of meeting would not be tolerated. And were told again. On the morning of the meeting, the Chinese gathered by the thousands. The Japanese calmly pulled the covers off the machine guns, which had been placed on roofs of the buildings around the square, and started firing, killing hundreds. Needless to say, the Chinese rapidly dispersed and didn't assemble ever again while under the watchful eye of the Nipponese.

When will the people who are leading our country, learn our all-loving God disciplines even His people? As it is said in Ecclesiastes 8:11, "Because the sentence against an evil deed is not executed quickly" may lead one to believe discipline is not forthcoming as it is dispensed when jumping from a cliff, but beware and believe any nation which follows the social behaviorism of Babylon will be disciplined or destroyed.

Someone once said "You're not ready to live until you learn to die." There are no truer words than these. And these words helped create for me the "World Within."

CHAPTER 11

The Void

As we descended deeper and deeper into the vast void, which 80 percent of the world's population experiences, known as starvation, we became cognizant of a great loss. Gradually, the facade of civilization dissipated from our nature. It seemed to leave day by day, nothing filling the void except the gnawing hunger. It seemed we became a spiritual being rather than a natural being.

Unless a person has experienced long-term starvation, they cannot grasp the devastating effect on the inner being. All of the learned niceties such as courtesies, personal and public hygiene, laws, consideration, social structures, and hate, wither and die.

The only element to survive the devastation is love of God and family. Love of God was continually with me and I knew, beyond doubt, He must have paradise in store for us. Love of family occupied my thoughts at times. It was about this time, I discovered and entered into the practice of "Remote Mind Control" for want of a better name. This was the practice of filtering every thought through the RMC and discarding any thought from your consciousness except those dealing with the acceptance of death and the love of the Creator and His resurrection of the human soul.

Our president has recently started a war with Iraq. On television, the young troops and their loved ones were wondering how you keep your morale boiling during the shock of battle and pre-battle jitters. I know the avenue to sustaining life is well said by Oswald Chambers[5] when, "Most of us live on the borders of consciousness—consciously serving, consciously devoted to God. All this is immature, it is not the real life yet. The mature stage is the life of a child which is never conscious; we become so abandoned to God that the consciousness of being used never enters in. . . . " To survive the days and nights and months and years, of deprivation, suffering and starvation, I, and most of the rest of the prisoners, abandoned the worldly world, and turned ourselves over to God for his final judgment call. Yes, we were as children again. We had nothing, we expected nothing and we lived unconsciously from moment to moment. It is very difficult for me to conjure up words to properly describe the feelings in the depths of my soul, but I guess one way to put it, is to say a deep contentment enveloped me as I blotted out the worldly thoughts and dreams, practicing my ever present RMC. I don't remember saying prayers daily or on the spur of the moment, for it seemed with total abandonment, prayers were not necessary.

Total abandonment to God is something the troops, in the Saudi desert war of today, need as their armor when going into battle, or placating the anxieties of pre-battle stress.

The winter of 1942–43 was not as harsh as the previous winter. Maybe we were more acclimated or our bodies were getting used to the deprivation and starvation. In the bad weather, and Southern China can really have terrible weather, we polished artillery shells for the Japanese. Of course, this was strictly forbidden by the Geneva Convention relative to the Treatment of Prisoners of War. If you even mentioned this Convention, the Nip you were talking to would clobber the hell out of you.

I believe I forgot to mention previously, but all of Southern China smells like a cesspool filled with human excrement. In fact, when you are 20 miles at sea, you can smell China. I imagine the seagoing vessels, at night and in storms, can tell easily when they are within landfall.

We received a Red Cross parcel on Christmas 1942, from the International Red Cross of Geneva, Switzerland. I don't want anyone to get the idea any help came from the American Red Cross. The prisoners of war with me had a very repulsive experience with the American Red Cross and I have never forgiven the ARC, or given them a nickel since WW II, nor will I contribute to any organization which in turn donates to the American Red Cross, such as the United Fund. All the time I was a prisoner, my parents gave enormous amounts of money to the American Red Cross. They also were assured by the American Red Cross any packages which parents wanted to send to the prisoners would be securely handled and delivered by them or their representatives.

I never received one package through any effort of the American Red Cross. When I and a thousand other prisoners were taken to Guam in 1945, from Japan, we had no money whatsoever. At the field hospital, we were told, provided we would go to this certain location tent, we could get some money from the American Red

Cross. We all headed down there. Upon our arrival, the American Red Cross representative agreed to let each of us have ten dollars, provided we signed a promissory note in which we promised to pay the money back when we reached the States. They even wanted to charge us for coffee and doughnuts. We told them to go to hell in no uncertain terms.

We went down a couple of tents to the Salvation Army, who gave us ten dollars with no strings attached, plus all the free donuts and coffee we could consume. I imagine you can guess who I give my donations to, ever since that day so long ago.

Anyway, back to the International Red Cross parcel. We received three of these packages during my tenure as prisoner. Two in China and one in Japan. The International Red Cross (IRC) sent enough of these scrumptious bundles for each Japanese prisoner to enjoy one per week. The German prisoners I talked to after the war said they received them as regularly as weekly. The Japanese stored them in warehouses as they received them from the IRC. Tons of them were found by our troops in warehouses after the war was over.

The reasons given for not distributing the packages to the prisoners were various, such as: one, the Japanese propaganda machine couldn't very well tell their people they were winning the war with the prisoners living like fat capitalistic pigs and smoking American cigarettes at work. Two, they might need the food for their troops provided the China Seas blockade by the Allies shut down the inflow of food from the China mainland. Three, the ruling body was enjoying the goodies and selling much of the IRC food on the black market. My folks told me after the war, they sent me a personal food parcel each month which would include such articles as Bull Durham, handmade boots, handmade woolen socks, long handles, razors, toothbrush and paste, sweaters, Levis and many other items suitable for prison camp comfort. I never received a solitary personal package, and neither did any other prisoner in the camps where I was confined.

The IRC parcels were a superb model of planning ingenuity. Each item fit its own little space in the box perfectly. Some of the items were: two packs of cigarettes (usually Chesterfields or Camels, never Lucky Strikes. I believe all production of Lucky Strikes was going to the free troops), a can of powdered milk (one make was Royal Canadian which was the creamiest and traded at a premium price; I have never seen it on the market since then), several Hershey bars, cheese, cookies or hardtack, several types of C rations (ham, eggs, etc.); a can of corn willy or fish, and undoubtedly items I can't remember.

Thievery ran rampant when an IRC shipment came into the compound. It was so bad we had to either make the barracks off-limits to all prisoners during the working hours or appoint a prisoner guard (and the prisoner guards were suspect when something was missing and if the Nips didn't kill the a--holes we told them we would kill them ourselves) to stay in each section to guard the premises. I am not sure how the officers were able to talk the Nips into giving us permission to leave the prisoner guards off the work details because they dare not stipulate we had thieves in our midst, for this sin required the death penalty.

You may wonder how long a parcel would last a prisoner. Normally, when supplementing the barley ration, an IRC parcel was meant to last a week. However, some prisoners would take each item out of the parcel box at mealtime and fondle item by item, never eating a bit of the parcel food, only the barley ration. They would keep the IRC food for years. This is an example of what "starvation" can do to a "civilized" person.

Of course, after a couple of weeks, if the IRC food was not eaten, the prisoner guards were removed and you had to carry your hoard with you at all times, even when you went to potty at night.

There was one event which caused great laughter in the compound. The incident happened after I was sent to Kawasaki, Japan, in 1943.The Allied air raids started in the spring of 1945, and we had received an IRC parcel about three months previously. One night, when the air raid siren sounded, we all took off for the railroad underpass used as an air raid shelter. One of the prisoners had hoarded his IRC parcel and carried it with him to the shelter. Well, some creative character had fashioned an IRC replica out of wooden blocks and bricks; and had placed them in an IRC box to ensure they all were the proper size. The "thief," and I use the word lightly, sat next to the hoarder in the dark tunnel.

During the three or four hours we were in the shelter, the "thief" transferred each unit out of the "hoarder" box thru a slit, replacing each unit with the replica. After we returned to the prison, we heard the "hoarder" yelling he had been robbed. Needless to say, no one felt the least compassion for the "hoarder." He never did find out who robbed him. People carried totes with their valuables (hoarded boiled barley, if you can imagine such an item being valuable) in them, to and fro from the shelters, so it was easy for the "thief" to disguise the incoming tote.

CHAPTER 12

Spring of '42

Along in April 1942, the balmy, soft days of spring came to the Yangtze River Delta and with spring came the wonderful sunny days which will warm a man's innards, and even though his guts are empty, his spirits are lifted.

The springtime of 1942 reminded me of the spring shown in *Dr. Zhivago* when he and his little girl along with his wife went to live in the country.

I remember the first warm, sunny, marvelous spring day, when we crawled out of our winter hibernation and sat down next to the barracks in the sunshine on the east side. I laid my head on my knees and thanked the Lord for bringing me through the long, depressing, cold winter days of "No-Where-Land and No-Nothing-Life." During the winter, the section was given a bible by the International Red Cross. We read it extensively during our hibernation that winter and with 32 pairs of hands thumbing it daily, the print was practically worn from the pages.

I think it was this time on the luscious, sunny day, I gave my life to God and, in faith, knew if I didn't make it through this hell on earth, He would take me "home" to paradise as the Lord Jesus promised. My grandchildren, when reading this, will probably consider the above to be a shallow assertion, but in their lifetime when the going gets tough & rough (and it will, mark my word) and they have no one to console them nor will puny man and his Babylonian materialism satisfy their needs, then the assertion will become profound.

By this time, the prisoners had accepted the routine of the Nip guards trouncing them with clubs for no reason at all. When you were standing at attention for muster or other occasions, a guard would walk up to you and whack you on the head with his club. Then he would yell at you in their usual gibberish and then clobber you again because you didn't respond properly to a language barrier.

Another of the Nips' favorite disciplinary actions was tying a prisoner to a chair, forcing a rubber hose down his throat and pouring water into his stomach until he was unconscious or dead.

Another . . . to punish the entire section for one person's theft or other violation of rules. A section would be selected at random, and spend the night at attention with no food, but work as usual the next day. Whatta life!

There was a tremendous amount of stealing or theft all during the four years of imprisonment and someone always received an inhumane beating for the crime, guilty or not.

Around the middle of April 1942, the Nips started organizing work details. I was assigned to go on one of the various "road gangs."

During the time I was on the road gang, we walked hundreds of miles, all over the delta, from Shanghai to the ocean. We got up at six a.m., went to benjo, had muster, ate our bowl of steamed barley and drank a cup of hot water, mustered outside, picked up our shovel or other tool, and marched off to repair the Chinese freeways of the day. Some prisoners operated the yea-ho equipment, which consisted of a pole, two prisoners, and a straw basket . . . or the configuration may be a pole, one prisoner and two straw baskets, according to the temperament of the guard on any certain day.

If you guessed the baskets held bricks of dirt when the road equipment was in operation, you guessed correctly and go to the head of the class. Usually the "gang" consisted of 30 or 40 prisoners. We eventually were able to hike 20 miles a day and never miss a beat, and work for six hours, returning to the compound at seven p.m. We weighed in at about 110 pounds per body. It would astound you what your body can withstand when the proper discipline is applied thereon.

The only days you didn't work in the entire visit to the Greater Co-Prosperity Sphere was the Emperor's birthday (April 29) and Christmas (December 25). The Japanese are a wonderfully religious nation. I have often speculated as to what the world will be spiritually and naturally, if and when the Japanese turn to Christianity, and what the United States could be, provided they would follow in the footsteps of the Nips. Glory be!

Along in May of '42, we commenced the great "farm" experiment. The Nips arranged to take over about 40 acres of farmland next to our compound. I believe they call the acquisition of land in this fashion "confiscation" and I think the power of the sword had something to do with success. The land belonged to a Chinese village and had a great number of burial mounds dotting the landscape.

Earlier in this treatise, I mentioned a man named "Gunner," a huge Swede or Scandinavian of some kind or other. He was the one responsible for digging Moon and I out from the overflow of our personal bomb blast on Wake Island.

Gunner had, at some time, been exposed to farming for he was responsible regarding the success of our bean farm. The International Red Cross acquired several hundred shovels from somewhere and sent them to the Woosung Forts.

Gunner positioned about 300 prisoners abreast at the east end of the 40 acres, with shovels and told us we would turn over the earth to a depth of 24 inches. He figured the Chinese, for thousands of years, had been turning the soil to a depth of ten to twelve inches, and thus the subsoil should be very rich in nutrients. In addition, the Chinese continually spread their human excrement on the land which added additional nutrients to the land. The Yangtze River had deposited luscious humus on this land for time immemorial. The river also flooded about every spring, depositing additional prime soil on the delta.

We started shoveling and shoveling and shoveling. I am reminded of the little character "Pac-Man," chomping and chomping as we devoured the field and the graves of the long-gone Chinese ancestors.

The graves would disgorge various pottery and jewelry. Of course, this was confiscated for the benefit of the "Greater Co-Prosperity Sphere."

Eventually the field was completely plowed. Then came the task of "harrowing." The Nips scrounged some timbers about the size of two by eights. Then Gunner procured some railroad spikes somewhere. We drove the spikes through several timbers and fastened them together to make a harrow. With four or five men standing on the harrow and a team of sixteen to twenty men pulling on straw lines, the field was smoothed ready to plant. We had four teams, so each team alternated every fourth trip down the 40 acres. And it worked.

The International Red Cross furnished us with enough beans to plant the field, a little reddish-brownish bean I had never seen before or since. I was chosen as one of the men to plant. You couldn't trust everyone to not eat the beans, and it was made specifically clear that if you were caught in any kind of a chewing motion, facially speaking, you may or may not live to regret the action. You were to plant each bean as if it were a personality all its own, to a depth of the first knuckle and eight inches apart. During the growing season, the farm was well patrolled, in the daytime by Gunner and by night, the Nips.

Well, the farm was a huge success, producing a bumper crop of several tons of those delicious little devils. They were the mealiest, sweetest little morsels God ever created. The only trouble being the Nips controlled the ration to the extent where we still only received our usual 600-800 calories per day, and of course, the Nips ate or sold an untold amount of the crop.

The seed crop for the 1943 growing season was withheld and planted in that year. I was not there to enjoy the '43 crop but I heard it was an immense success, also.

The International Red Cross, in 1942, shipped into Woosung Fort a number of goats. Their milk was reserved for the sick and dying prisoners. The goats needed a reserve supply of hay for the winter months, and thus I was blessed with the best job of any I enjoyed in the four years of internment. I was assigned to the "hay detail." Actually, when I think back over those years and the tasks on which I labored, I was usually assigned to a job because it appeared to the men in charge it would be a shit detail but this detail materialized into the best under the circumstances. I loved the hay detail. There were only five men on the detail, one honcho and four coolies. I was a coolie. We were on the "honor system," and we could go anywhere within sight of the forts without a guard, and work at our own pace.

We had hand scythes, a bale-shaped wooden box and plenty of straw rope for tools. We had a two-wheeled cart (known as a "yaka") to haul the tied bales into camp. The sequence of production was cut the grass, stuff it in the box, trample it with feet, and tie into a bale. It was wonderful to be out in the fields with no guard around. We could scour the land for wild onions, volunteer crops of peanuts, rice and daikons. Also, we could wade for crawdads in the drain ditches. Of course, all the time we were exploring for food, we had to keep cutting hay. The days were wonderful after the horror of the winter hibernation, and some of the fearful beatings in the barracks. I don't do too well mentally, unless I can fight back. I pray I can watch my back trail adequately so as to never be subjugated again in this life.

We were able to stay out in the field all day by hauling all the bales in at the close of the work day. This enabled us to take a little nap in the sunshine at noon after we would eat a small amount of barley saved from breakfast. I was on the hay detail until late in the fall of 1942.

On the route of the march to work on one work project, each day we would pass through a small village. This village had a number of families in it and they'd all turn out *en masse* to see the "foreigners." The people were always sublimely happy; laughing and playing grab-ass with each other. In fact, I don't remember any group of people in the United States ever being this cheerful day in and day out. They worked in the fields every day of the year, and their main diet consisted of vegetables and rice. They had enough clothes to cover their bodies and wore shoes made of fabric in the wintertime. Some of the women were stunning and a majority of the men were attractive. I can specifically remember a gorgeous girl with red hair (I suspect a redheaded marine may have been in her ancestry at some point in history) and her complexion and figure were flawless. The people were reasonably clean, especially in the summertime when they were scantily-dressed; otherwise their clothing covered most of their body. But the characteristic I remember vividly was their happiness.

After I was taken to Japan in 1943 and forced to labor among the people of Japan, I saw the same inherent happiness in the faces and lives of the Japanese, and even the conscript laboring Koreans.

These people of the Far East have lived in contentment and happiness for thousands of years. I fervently believe it is arrogance of the Western nations to contend these people will be more content and happy under the West's so-called capitalistic democracies. The definition of civilization entertains the thought of "to cause to develop out of a primitive state. . ."[6] From my experience in the world of life and business during the last 45 years, I regard the Western civilization as being regressive rather than developmental.

Walk down the street in any city in the Western world and note, if any, the people smiling or laughing or better yet, try going along a street among a crowd, grinning and laughing to yourself as you walk; you will notice the people staring at you as if you are completely crazy. I know because I research it from time to time to get a reaction. Nowadays, if you smile at a person of the opposite sex, you are reported for "sexual harassment."

I have noted an analogy between the concepts of the Western Capitalistic Democracies and the theme of the bible. Throughout the bible, God and his prophets speak of the Messiah and the continuing plague on humans called Satan. I am inclined to believe the unpretentious civilizations such as the pre–World War II Chinese and Japanese are the Godly influence in the world and Western civilization is the presence of Satan coming to fruition after the Resurrection and before the Second Coming.

CHAPTER 13

Kiangwan

In the late summer of 1942, the Nip Management Association decided we, about 500–600 prisoners, would build a shrine to the Japanese people. Of course, the Nips owned all of China so they had no problem getting the land for the shrine. The site was about six to eight miles south of the Kiangwan prison camp, where we had been transferred from the Woosung camp in the summer of 1942.

This camp wasn't too far from the old camp at Woosung. I never did know why the Nips transferred us to the Kiangwan camp. Anyway, I was transferred off the hay detail, much to my dismay, and told to join the shrine movement. The prisoners soon called the shrine-to-be "Mt. Fuji," by reason whereas we were to dig a hole about four acres square and ten feet deep and carry the dirt up to the adjacent four acres and stack it up. When finished, Mt. Fuji was to be a mountain from which you could look out and see a lake created by the hole from whence the mountain came.

During the time we were building the Mt. Fuji, we lost quite a few men. A sailor friend of mine was electrocuted on the fence surrounding the prison. Also, a couple of guys were killed by the "Water Treatment." The water treatment was punishment for just about anything from stealing a bowl of barley to not understanding Japanese when told to do something by a guard. As stated before, they would stick a hose down your throat and pour water into your stomach until you became unconscious or died. Also a number of men died from tuberculosis, dysentery, pneumonia, and starvation.

Anyway, we would get up about six a.m., crap, count off, eat our cup of barley, and start the march to Fuji. This went on every day of the year except the Emperor's birthday or Christmas day. With 500 dysentery-prisoners marching along a dirt road, you can imagine how many were falling out to take a crap continually. There were always Chinese farmers (men and women) working the fields along the way and they didn't blink an eye when a prisoner stopped and crapped right in front of them.

It took us about two hours to get to Fuji, walking four abreast. Then we would work from about nine a.m. until about five p.m. and then head back to camp.

Daily, we went through a pretty good-sized Chinese village on the way to and from Fuji. Every time we went through the village, the Chinese would line the road, giggling and laughing at us. At the time of their rice harvest, they'd lay mats down in the road where we'd be walking, and on the mats they'd place the rice bundles which they'd harvested from their fields. As we'd march by, walking on top of the bundles, we'd thresh their grain for them, and it was death to the prisoner who'd bend over and pick up any of the rice. The Chinese and the Japanese always seemed to have plenty of food to eat.

To build Mt. Fuji, we had shovels, and originally, carried the dirt up the hill in straw baskets on a pole. With two men to a pole.

In the fall of 1942, the Nips brought in a bunch of railroad tracks. Not the ordinary gauge railroad, but this type was made to use in mines, narrow gauge. Also they had small cars which ran on the tracks and would carry about a square yard of dirt. Four men were assigned to a cart. At first, the tracks ran straight up and down Mt. Fuji. After the hill started to have some height to it, the tracks were connected to form one huge circle. The problem with the circle was that all teams had to work at the same speed or many teams would be waiting on the slow ones. Some of the prisoners would lay back, I was one of them, and push the patience of the Nips to the breaking point. Louie and I always believed we should accomplish as little as possible for the "Greater Co-Prosperity Sphere of East Asia." Some prisoners and "honchos" worked like hell for them. The hotshots were always mad at our team for holding up the production. The Nips must have thought we were a bunch of nuts. They would give us a quota of trips per day and we were told our food ration would be cut or terminated provided we didn't make the quota. We knew the only trouble with a quota system was the quota increases as the worker meets the quota. Most of the prisoners agreed we should not accommodate the Nips in their endeavors to make their colonel, who was our camp commander, look good for the visiting dignitaries.

Anyway, Louie and I caused them as much grief as possible and said "to hell" with the guys who cooperated in the building of the shrine. There were a few days when we would be punished with half rations. But half of nothing still isn't very much, and as long as you are starving, a little more pain isn't all so noticeable.

There were certain members of my section who were always trying to convince me to abandon my friendship with Louie. They said I was a good worker when I wasn't influenced by him.

The Nips brought many dignitaries to the camp to show off the Allied prisoners of war. Most of them were military people and, once in a while, a governor of some conquered province or country.

Sometimes, the International Red Cross would get as far as the main gate but were never allowed to talk to anyone in the camp but our officers. Of course, the Nip interpreter was always present during any of these reviews and, I suspect, if or when the officer said what was on his mind, we all would pay through reduced rations or an all-night, stand-at-attention, vigil with the moon. Also, I suspect some of the officers would not describe the true conditions of internment to protect their own skins. They were getting all the food they could eat, and in addition, were never on a work detail. It was on the work details where 80 percent of the beatings, or the skull rappings, occurred, so you can imagine how many cracks on the head the officers received.

I can still remember, after all these 50 years, how I hated the Nips when they would hit us with a club or gun butt and then smirk as if daring us to give them the provocation to stick a bayonet in our gut. I know now it is far better for my mental health to think of such mental images as little as possible. However, this is very difficult, when the society in which we live continually brings to memory injustices every moment of the day. As Oswald Chambers states in his book, "I have to learn that the aim in life (my life) is God's not mine. God is using me from His great personal standpoint, and all He asks of me is that I trust Him, and never say . . . 'Lord, this gives me such heartache. . . '"[7] I have to elevate myself from the natural "world" to the spiritual "world." This is why I must live in a "World Within" a world.

The years in the various camps now seem to have been a monstrous nightmare, and although I didn't consciously admit to my natural being when I was constantly relying on God's strength to bring me through, I know in living the squalid and sordid existence, I had continually moved in God's protective embrace, looking only to Him for my deliverance and salvation wherever He may lead me; whether in this world of worlds or eternity.

CHAPTER 14

Hades by the Sea

Along in the spring of 1943, the Nips gave all military men aptitude examinations (I don't know how they picked the prisoners, for later I learned some military men missed the exercise). When you're a prisoner, you're not quite sure what the purpose of the exam will be. Just maybe all of those passing the exam will be executed. So, you're caught between a rock and a hard place, not knowing what you should do. Anyway, I decided to do the best I could and trust in God as to the path of my future. I believe man continually strives to achieve wise decisions through his ignorance, when actually, provided he will leave the heavy decisions to God, the future will be brighter.

I never knew what happened to the results of the exam, but in a couple of weeks (in August 1943), I was listed among 100 men, to go to some undisclosed destination. If you don't think an announcement such as this will bring your spirits crashing to the bottomless pits, you should try it sometime under like circumstances. The only thing I had to take with me was my rice bowl and my cup which were both in a little cloth bag. My little bag was so filthy it could stand alone and substitute for a waste basket. I guess you could call such as "traveling light."

I never did understand, but for the next week, during our travels to the "undisclosed destination," the Nips seemed almost human.

The day we left the camp, some trucks pulled up to the main gate and we were told to load up. We had always walked everywhere we ventured in the past. Riding was a luxury unheard of in the vernacular of the POW. The trucks took us down to the docks near Shanghai and stopped beside a small intercoastal ship (which I later believed to be named the *Murote*). I would say about a 2000-ton ship.

We were told to get aboard and the guards took us down into the hold of the ship. But the hatch was not battened down, nor were we given any instructions about our movements in the hold, only we could not go on deck without permission. Now you could have knocked us over with a feather. At first we were certain the war was over, and then the outreach conclusions began to fill our thoughts; such as, maybe this is a new method of eliminating the POWs and we would soon be killed and thrown overboard as had happened to many, many prisoners.

The ship got under way the same evening. The evening meal was out of this world. It was a stew of a sorts, with nice white rice and a reasonable ration. It had to be the same food the crew was eating.

We wondered if this was to be our last meal. We were uneasy when we lay down in the hold to sleep that night, to say the least. However, God's day broke over the sea as usual and we had rice for breakfast. I neglected to say earlier, but I was the only one from my section in Kiangwan prison who was aboard the ship. I was never to see my friend "Louie" again.

Then as the day progressed, to our great astonishment, we were allowed to go up on the "weather" deck in the beautiful ocean-going sunshine and walk around. If you have never been to sea and bathed in the luxury of the sun in the salt air, you have missed one of God's most exquisitely created moments of life on this earth.

Instead of reveling in the moment, we were all so suspicious, we didn't fully appreciate the opportunity of the freedom and extravagance being offered at the time, albeit unknowingly by the ship's captain.

Also, instead of buckets in the hold to be used as toilets, we were allowed to go to "benjo" in the ship's heads or johns. The ship we were traveling on was a merchant marine. The johns were built on platforms, out over the side of the ship (out over the gunnel). The total supporting structure was made of wood and held to the side of the ship by hemp lines. When you were in the structure, you used a slot in the floor to straddle and your excrement dropped into the ocean. If battle stations were sounded, a crew member merely cut the lines and the john and anyone in it, fell into the ocean. I remember each time I stepped into one of the little houses, I said a little prayer asking the Supreme Being to command any U.S. submarine skipper to please postpone any torpedo exercise for at least 20 minutes to half an hour.

In a couple of days, we were in the lower islands off Honshu and they were absolutely gorgeous after the stench and level land of the Yangtze Delta.

We landed in Yokohama and were transferred at night to a train which was to take us to our destination. I remember seeing the people, both men and women, in the streets. They were very curious as to who we were and I imagine we were a sad looking bunch with the heaviest weighing in at about 120 pounds. I had never seen the cultural dress of Japan before and I remember how beautiful the women looked with all of their black long hairdos and beautiful clothes. Most of the men wore a pseudo-military suit. Actually the contact with the population was rather exhilarating and little did we know of the hellhole we were about to enter.

We rode the train a short while and then disembarked only to use the shanks' ponies (our own feet) the rest of the way to the Kawasaki Camp, where we were to exist until May 1945.

The Kawasaki Camp was right on the edge of metropolitan Tokyo and right across a main thoroughfare from probably the largest steel mill in Japan. I am not sure of the name of the mill now but then it was Nippon Steel. It must have covered several thousand acres of land right on Tokyo bay. The prison was built of lumber and huge timbers, being held together with U-shaped staples so the building could sway during earthquakes.

In the two years I was held in the prison at Kawasaki, we had dozens of tremors and it seemed after a while the quakes were commonplace, stirring little comment or excitement. The interior of the building was built in bays with approximately 24 prisoners per bay. Each bay was double-decked. In two separate buildings outside were a bath house and the galley. Sometimes the bath house had warm water but usually not and always no soap.

The compound was used to house conscript labor (usually Koreans) before the advent of World War II. We were to work in the Nippon Steel Mill with civilian guards and civilian laborers. It was not long before we were to wish we were back in China with the military for guards.

The "Big Cheese" or boss of the prison was a character named "Kondo." He was pretty good size for a Nip; about five feet ten inches and 160 pounds. He was nothing but pure, unadulterated meanness. The guard whom I drew on the work parties, most of the time, was "Sato." Sato for the most part wasn't too bad, but once in a while his wife must have denied him, because he would beat the hell out of me for no reason whatsoever.

Our food at Kawasaki was mainly barley and it always had a musty smell. We received the same ration as we did in China but when we worked a full twelve hour shift, we would get a lunch to take into the mill with us. I can't remember working anything but twelve hour shifts.

The prison had about 100 men in it when we arrived from China. With our quota the prison held about 270 prisoners and stayed at the 270 level until May 1945; give or take a few guys dying now and then.

The men who were already in the prison, when I arrived there, were mostly from the Philippines and most of them had gone through the Bataan Death March. Boy, the Bataan March was truly something. To hear them talk about the "March" was an experience one would never forget. They were in such bad shape they looked like ghouls returning from the dead. They had been at the prison about three months when we arrived. As I said previously, we had no soap available whatsoever. When you worked in the steel mill, the smoke from the furnaces and the steel impregnates your skin, thus causing you to look as if you are at the cutting edge of death. Huge black circles under your eyes and every wrinkle emphasized with the grime and believe you me, a person who has lost half of his body weight does have wrinkles. Thus when I viewed the Philippine troops, I saw an image of my future self personified, thinking, "How can I survive living in these circumstances, unless God carries me through on his shoulders?"

Since then, I have come to realize the Father will never ask anything of me I cannot endure. I was in a trance for days after we arrived in Kawasaki.

The major sections of the mill where the prisoners of war were to work consisted of Joko, Grinders, Rollers and the Pipes. There was a small, one-man operation to which I was assigned as the lone prisoner of war and there were two Nipponese on the operation. It was called "Ichikan." There were numerous small work parties which would change their working complement day after day but generally most of the prisoners worked on the above four huge operations.

The mill's major commodities of production were reinforcing bar steel, ribbon steel, and pipes. In Ichikan, dies were used to expand and swell the end of the pipe to enable another male pipe to fit inside the female end of the pipe (I don't know what in the world we would do for a descriptive segment of our language if it were not for the terms "male" and "female").

One of the Nips chased the bundles of pipe with an overhead crane to supply our operation, while the other Nip and I ran the press and die machine. A blast furnace was part of our operation with the pipe-chaser loading the cold pipe into the mouth of the furnace. The Nip ran the press, which was energized by steam, while I fed the pipe into the press and unloaded the finished product. My guard was the character named "Sato" mentioned above, and between the two Nips on the machine and Sato, I was only knocked around about once a week. Sometimes I would be sick as an "old brown dog" and wouldn't have the strength to pull the pipe out of the press; consequently, during these times Sato or the two-striper Nip would slap me around. At times like these my hatred virtually consumed my soul.

The Nips who worked in the mill, along with hundreds of Koreans, were civilians. To differentiate authority, the workers wore billed caps with stripes designating the line of command.

Except for the foundry maintenance prisoners of war, I was the only one who worked alone with a Nip. I never did understand how I was selected for this appointment. I worked on Ichikan for about eight months and then was transferred to the foundry maintenance operation. The mill ceased to operate Ichikan for some reason.

Except for a very short period, maybe a couple of months, I always worked the day shifts. The foundry maintenance was probably the best task I had during my stay in Kawasaki.

When I went to work on the foundry detail, I was assigned to a Nip who was probably 55 years old, named "Pop," or at least "Pop" was the name the prisoners of war gave him. He was one of the better

Nips whom I met "over there." He never did beat me and in fact, tried to be halfway decent to me. Sato was always sneaking around and every so often, just to let me know I shouldn't forget I was a prisoner of war, would sneak up and whale-the-devil out of me.

Pop had a little two-wheeled cart known as a "yaka," which we would load up every morning with bricks, sand and cement and I would pull it to some steel blast kiln needing a new inside fire wall. We would tear out the old wall and build a new one.

While I was on the furnace detail, I started boiling seawater down in a pot until the residue produced salt or a product which re-sembled salt. The product also had a trace of iodine in it. I sold some of it and ate it on my barley. The Nips were really short on salt and when they discovered what we were doing, they started a regular explosion of salt production. I'll bet somebody made a lot of money on the salt gimmick.

Every once in a while, the Nips would get a ration of sweet pota-toes. The old man (Pop) for whom I was working would save the peelings for me. Lord, but they tasted wonderful.

Cigarettes were scarce to nonexistent in all prison camps, and Kawasaki was no exception. One day, on the way to the kiln, I bent over to "shoot a snipe" (pick up a cigarette butt) and Pop noticed the action. If you had quality butts, you could barter for food rations. Well, a couple days later when Sato wasn't around (the civilians didn't dare be caught fraternizing with the prisoners of war when he was), Pop guided the two of us on a detour when going home from work, through an alley where I had never been before. He pointed to a five-gallon can by a back door, which led to somewhere, then he went in the door and I could hear voices inside the building. When I approached the can, I could see it was half full of butts. I stuffed my ditty-bag, barley dish and coat with as many butts possible. Soon after I stashed all the butts I could carry, Pop came out with a grin on his face. I've often wondered if the door led to a cathouse. I picked up the yaka yoke, and we continued back to the prison gate. Needless to say, I ate fairly well for several days. I was never able to return to the unknown back door again, and I could never find anyone who knew what was behind the door in the building.

With the night shift working twelve hours and the day shift the same, provided you had something of value which needed to be guarded while you were gone, it was necessary for you to have a friend(s) on the opposite shift; each day the valuables must be carted down to the friend's bunk for safekeeping.

The following episode I call "Medals Ain't for Cowards." I had a friend from Boise, Idaho, who I met in China and who I'll call "Zeke." Zeke is probably the bravest man I have ever known. One time when I was working with Pop, I dropped the yaka, which is a two-wheel cart used to carry everything from soup to pig iron in Japan, loaded with firebrick on my ankle, causing terrible pain. I couldn't walk on it. Sato came up and started the "old club exercise" on my back, when Zeke came running up and grabbed me, lifting me into the yaka. Zeke then started off toward the prison main gate with me in the yaka. He could very easily have been killed for his brave effort.

When we arrived at the prison, Zeke helped me into the barracks, with Kondo, the big cheese, telling him to take me to the office. In the office, Kondo grabbed my ailing foot and started twisting it at the ankle with me yelling. Zeke reached over and stopped Kondo physically. He could have been shot on the spot for his bravery, but he bluffed Kondo out. I could never thank Zeke enough for what he did on that certain day so long ago. What a man . . . Zeke is at least six feet six inches tall, so you can imagine what poor health he has had as a result of eating the same size ration of food I was getting (I'm five feet ten). Also, he is ten years older than I am.

If anyone deserved a medal out of the Wake Island fracas, it is men such as Zeke, and not the officers who were running the show.

We had an American Indian, named Yellowhair, with us in Kawasaki. The guy seemed to always be in trouble with the Nips. He could not help himself when it came to food. He was continually stealing food from somewhere. The Nips would put him in their guardhouse which was inside of our prison compound. Within a day, Yellowhair would break out of their guardhouse and escape from our prison compound. Then the Nips would catch him as far as five miles away breaking into some food warehouse. The guy must have had a nose like a bloodhound, for he instinctively knew which building the food sources were stored in. Every time they caught him stealing food, they would bring him back to camp, tie him to a whipping post and beat the living hell out of him. I have seen the guy with blood running out of every orifice of his body. He must have had at least twenty of these beatings during the time I knew him. I really don't know how he ever lived through it all, but he did.

I have recently read in one of my Wake Island Bulletins, Steven (Chief) Yellowhair died in Wakpamni Lake, North Dakota, on February 6, 1991. He had four daughters and seven sons and he, himself, was a great grandson of the famous grandson of the famous Chief Sitting Bull.

A couple of nights, they put me on Joko. This was an operation where a huge table made of steel was laid on the floor of a steel building. I would guess the floor to be 200 yards long and 100 yards wide. In the middle of this huge table sat a long line of compression rollers with each set, two to a set, having a hole in the center between the two rollers, with each adjacent set having a more restrictive opening then the previous set. Prisoners worked on each side of the rollers with tongs. Into the first set of rollers was fed a 500 kilo red-hot iron pig. This pig was grabbed by each successive POW and shoved back thru the adjacent set of restrictive rollers, thus squeezing the pig smaller and smaller each time of entry through successive rollers. At the same time the pig became longer and longer.

Eventually, the pig developed into a ribbon of steel, one quarter-inch thick, two inches wide, and 200 feet long. The pig was red-hot all during the process. As the pig was elongated the POW had to quickly insert his end into the next set of rollers, for the tail would be whipping up towards him. If he missed the insertion, he would be encircled by the tail of a red-hot steel ribbon resembling a snake's tail traveling 40 miles an hour and would administer a painful death. We had men killed by the snake of steel. I was fortunate to only stay on Joko a few days. From Joko, I was transferred to the Pipes.

The Pipe operation consisted of about 20 POWs and about 30 Korean women. We were to grind the burrs and impurities off the pipe ends before they went to an operation such as Ichikan. The women worked at one end of the Pipe operation and the POWs at the other end of the Pipes. We were not to fraternize with the women. I was on night shift all the time I was on the Pipes.

The Korean girl (I think she was about 20 and I was about 22 then) who worked the other end of my section of pipe would smile at me and I would smile or wink at her. She seemed to be really sweet. In a steel mill, the noise is always deafening so when I would knock on our pipe, she would feel the vibration and look at me. We would talk by hand-sign and several times she asked me if I was hungry. She would wrap a rice ball in some paper; then send it through the pipe by compressed air. We could pull the air hose off the portable grinder and blow things to each other through the pipes which were about 20 feet long. We never did get any closer than the length of the pipe. At break time, the girls went one way and the POWs went another. We were never caught by the guards, practicing our innocent young romance. I have often wondered whatever happened to the girl. Such are the affairs of the heart.

From the Pipes, I was transferred to the Grinders, where I remained all the rest of my days in Kawasaki. I worked only nights on the Grinders. Twelve on and twelve off.

When they pour steel pigs in a steel mill, the molten metal has impurities in it. This can be dirt, slag, other metal, or some portion may cool faster than the rest of the pig causing a rift. In the Grinders, our job was to sit on a huge grinder with a grinding wheel about two to three feet in diameter which was run by a series of belts and pulleys. We could lean on the grinder over a 500 to 1000-kilo pig and grind for twelve hours, grinding out the flaws. Usually, we timed it so we finished a pig a night shift. You had one break after about six hours into the shift. When you don't have much to eat or drink, you don't have to make many potty jaunts.

I was on the Grinders when I discovered "self-hypnosis." When I would find a comfortable position on the grinder frame, I would practice self-hypnosis. To hypnotize one's self, you must start flipping mental frames of thoughts through your consciousness in a progressively rapid rate until your consciousness is nothing but a blank blur or thought-scenes rolling at high speed. You are conscious of everything around you, but you will have no concept of time. I used to, for all practical purposes, spend hours on the grinder and never recall any of the time. You have to be careful where you hypnotize yourself for you must be somewhere or doing something which requires no conscious effort on your part. One time we were marching, and I hypnotized myself, the road turned and I almost fell in a huge hole. Another prisoner grabbed me before I was hurt or subject to the Nips' fun fest.

The longer we were in Kawasaki, the more the morale and physical well-being of the POWs declined. The barracks smelled like the stench of death and a number of men had met their God and more were getting ready to meet Him. One man next to me found a can of tuna in a trash heap and smuggled it into the barracks. He ate it, and the next morning when we tried to get him up for work, he was stone cold dead. Dysentery was getting to everyone. When Zeke would go out to the john, other POWs would have to go with him to push his guts back into his rectum. Many men, when they would bend over the slit-trench to crap, didn't have the strength to get up again and had to call for help. The beatings from the guards became more frequent. Even now when I try to remember my love for God and His Son, I can feel my blood boil with hate from the atrocities of war.

A fellow I'll call Charlie, one night told me to come up to his bunk. Charlie and I had become friends through work. When I crawled up to Charlie's upper bunk, he produced a hard-boiled hen's egg. He and I sat there and savored every morsel of it. I never did question where in the world he got the egg. I never saw Charlie again after Kawasaki.

Another time, a special buddy I'll call "M.Z.," told me to come down to his bay. When I got there, M.Z. broke out a Lucky Strike cigarette and four of us friends felt like we were in heaven. Does anyone wonder why men under such circumstances form bonds which will last for eternity?

It must have been in the fall of 1944, when we were going through the gate on our way to work, and I had my hands in my pockets for it was cold as hell. A guard hit me on my right collarbone, which had been broken three times before, and fractured it. I just favored the shoulder at work and in time it got well, though I had a bad time sleeping sometimes.

Another time, along in 1944, I had a cyst develop on my right pelvic joint. The cyst was right on the spot where the thigh bone joins the hip joint. It grew to the point where I couldn't walk. The Nips decided someone should do something. We had a young man who had some medical training. I never knew whether he was a doctor or a corpsman, but I think a corpsman. He had a scalpel but no other instruments of value. No anesthesia. No stitching equipment. No nothing.

They laid me on a wooden table, face down. One guy sat on my legs while another sat on my back. Then the doc stuck the scalpel four inches into the cheek of my butt, and out came the gushing poison and my yelling some foul, and I mean foul, language. Doc then took a wire, put a hook on the end of it, pushed it into the hole in my buttock and twisted to break the puss pocket. I thought I was dying and wished to God I could, but I didn't. Doc then stuck a large rice straw he had cut from the stubble in the field back of the compound, into the second asshole he had made in my derriere. I didn't have to work for a couple of days but I had to keep the straw in my buttocks for a couple of weeks. I looked funny walking around with the straw sticking out of the hole I cut in my pants. That's another experience I wouldn't care to go through again.

All of the POWs had dental problems. Your teeth would just rot away until you could pull the roots out by hand. We all kept a chunk of roofing tar handy, and when we started having a toothache, we would put a slug of tar over it, and presto, the ache would subside, to some extent.

For dysentery, diarrhea, worms, etcetera, we would take plain wood charcoal. The black charcoal was the only medicine I saw in the four prison years. We had worms so badly, you could feel them in your throat and actually reach down with your fingers and pull them out your mouth. I developed stomach ulcers while a prisoner and at times felt as if my pain would cause me to commit suicide. Also, from the beatings, I began to have blackouts. Maybe the malnutrition caused them. I had a touch of tuberculosis and a good case of malaria.

After going to Kawasaki, I developed beriberi and my legs would swell to twice their normal size. We had one fellow with beriberi whose waist went from 26 inches to 80 inches. He also went blind.

After you had worked in the steel mill for a few months, the one pair of pants and the jacket (tunic), which we had for clothes, were impregnated with filth. We had no soap but in the mill there was a huge barrel of fish oil which we could dip our clothes in. It actually took some of the dirt out but left a slimy film and the fish smell.

Now 50 years later, I wonder why, with all the beatings, starvation, ill health, frustration, etcetera, we even bothered to think of cleanliness. It was so futile. And the life in the United States was just a dismal dream, as unreachable as the planet Jupiter. The Lord only knows why but we still existed from day to wretched day.

THE SILVER ANGELS

From Whence They Came

From heaven they came
All shiny and bright,
As stars up in heaven
Which glow in the night.
They sailed thru the skies
To seek us and find,
And what did they see
But the dregs of mankind.
Why come they now
When man's hope is gone,
What does remain
For freedom's sweet song?
We only know
When their numbers increase,
Our prayers will be answered
For a spiritual feast
— dkk

(B-29 Bombers)

In the spring of 1945, we had a saying: "The Golden Gate in 48." About this time, we started seeing B-29s in their reconnaissance flights. We had no idea the United States had such monstrous airplanes. We would watch those big, silver beauties at about 35,000 feet with the sun glistening on them and the beautiful blue sky as a background, making a contrail from horizon to horizon. As I would watch the B-29s, I would fantasize I was up there flying the airplane, thinking of the ice-cold beer or sizzling steak which I would close my lips upon when the flight was over.

It was difficult to envision freedom was only 35,000 feet away even though it was straight up. And we also knew the life in the cockpit of one of the "Silver Angels" might as well have been on the moon for what little chance we had of experiencing the pilot's gifts of God. No matter what the Nip propaganda machine expounded, there would be an end to this horrible tragedy called "WAR," even though we may not be alive to see it.

From the time we spotted the first lone B-29 fly-over, the numbers of planes per day rapidly increased. After a few weeks, the B-29s began bombing the greater Tokyo metropolis during the night. The Nips had a no night-fighter airplanes. We would cease work at the sound of the air raid siren and go to a railroad underpass, which was close to our work and the prison compound.

Finally, in May 1945, we had a 500-plane raid, which scattered incendiary gelatin (napalm) bombs like a farm gal feeding chickens. The planes were so low we could see them in the light of the thousands of fires which were roaring from the gelatin menace. The carrier of the gelatin explodes at a pre-set altitude and throws the burning petroleum gel in all directions, adhering to anything which it touches. Ninety percent of Tokyo was built of paper and wood structures. Forty square miles of the city was on fire that specific night.

Seeing the huge fire cataclysm brought back the memories of when I was a boy in the summertime in Boise, Idaho. When the strawberries were on the market, they would be delivered from the strawberry farm in a crate called a flat. The flat would be filled with twelve small wooden cups called baskets. The kids around the neighborhood would gather the baskets from wherever and we would build a large city from them. You could make doors and windows and paint them to look like real buildings. Then at some predetermined time, usually at dusk, we would set the whole city on fire. WHOOOOOOSH!!!! Just like Tokyo on that night in 1945.

The huge fire heated the atmosphere and thus caused a pseudo-cyclone wind which, of itself, tore and demolished the human-built structures as if they were box matches and paper sacks. The raid must have lasted at least five hours (I had left my Rolls Reflex at home on the dresser). The fire departments and equipment were useless against such a wildfire. Our underpass bomb shelter started filling with water from broken fire mains. At one time during the night, we were certain the guards were going to leave us in the underpass and let us drown. Luckily the water was cut off somewhere after it was about three feet deep. Just one damn death-threatening episode after another. We thought, "Will death never come?"

At the end of the raid, we were marched back to the prison compound and were told to stand at attention. We were to stand in the yard at attention for two days and two nights with no food or water, as punishment for the damage the bombers had done to the city.

One thing happened which will always make me a believer of miracles and the power of the almighty God. The "gel bombs" had fired all the city around us, right up to the prison compound fence, which was even blackened by the fire, and then some "Power" greater than man stopped the holocaust. Do you know who that was? Not one splinter of our prison wall was burned!

After we completed our stint of standing at attention, we were formed into work parties and sent to the burned areas to start cleaning up the debris from the fire. A couple of our people were nearly beaten to death for writing "V for Victory" on the fire-blackened wall of a hospital, where hundreds of patients had been burned to death. It is untenable what people will do in the name of "patriotism." There were thousands of people killed by the wildfire during the night; men, women, children. Thus we say, "We are patriots and civilized humans."

WHERE HE LEADS

I arise each morn amid filth and squalor

And pray to the Lord with a soul in need,

And know not where God's angels lead,

I only know where He leads I follow.

— dkk

We worked for several weeks, cleaning up the bramble the wildfire left. One day we were marching down a road, and we could hear the drone of a lone American engine. We could always tell the difference between the American and Nip plane engines. As we looked to the rear of the column of men, we saw a P-51 emerge from the cloud bank which had been hanging over us all morning. We had never seen one before and knew not what type it was. He was heading straight at four large smoke stacks all in a row. We realized he would crash provided he continued on his current path, for he couldn't fly between the stacks.

Then all at once, he tipped the P-51 on its side and flew on towards us. Then his guns were firing at us so we all dove over a rock wall at the road's edge. One of the men lit in a "honey-pot"—a huge pot full of human excrement. It took us all day to clean him up. No one was hit by the strafing. We now knew the U.S. was closing in on the island of Honshu from the one fighter plane's appearance. *And we knew when the "LANDING" came we would all be massacred.*

One day, when on the wildfire cleanup detail, we came across a warehouse, in which had been stored thousands of cans of tomato puree, catsup or tomatoes. Most of the cans and cases were burned so badly you couldn't stand to eat the black crust the heat had formed. However, provided you dug down in the piles of cans far enough, you could find cans which were tolerable for consumption. The guards decided it was alright for us to eat what we could. I ate so much I became violently ill and my rectum, by the end of the day, resembled one of the discharge gates at Coulee Dam. Ever since the "day of the catsup," I can't stand catsup or Italian food cooked in tomato derivatives of any kind.

At the end of our assigned work at cleaning up the debris of the wildfire, we were told one day, to prepare to travel the next day (in May 1945), for we would be going to another prison. We had nothing to pack except our barley bowl and cup.

CHAPTER 15

Niigata by the Sea

In the Kawasaki Camp, we were located on Tokyo Bay, which is on the east side of the island of Honshu. The camp in Niigata would be on the China Sea which would be on the west side of Honshu.

On the day of transport, we were marched down to the train station (about 270 of us), and, lo and behold, instead of putting us in box cars, we were put in regular train passenger cars, with seats, windows, and Western-style toilets. We couldn't get over the toilets. I must have gone to the pot at least eight times during the eight hour trip, to enjoy the feeling of fantasy when I would close my eyes and dream I was in my folks' home.

Seems stupid now, for a grown man to be so unrealistic as to dream fantasies from the stimulus of a toilet seat.

Of course, we had guards at both ends of each rail car. When afternoon rolled around, the people who were running the train served us a box lunch. The POWs were joking, thinking the war must be over, judging from the treatment we were getting. The box lunch was delicious. It had soy grasshoppers, white rice, pickled kelp, and a small portion of fish. . . . Marvelous. . . . Superb.

During the four years of prison confinement, it seemed certain portions of Japan's populace forgot to "hate the Americans" as they were told to do by the military leaders or their government. The people on the train were as friendly as any American society and very courteous. But, this was not to last.

The camp at Niigata was about seven or eight miles east of the town proper. Actually, the country around the Niigata Camp was beautiful with some huge mountains on the east side of the valley. The China Sea was to the west of the town. There is a natural seaport at Niigata with a nice estuary. Most of the Siberian and Korean shipping use the Niigata port. The Niigata Prison Camp, with our 270, now carried about 1000 prisoners. We were reunited with many of the POWs we had left in China. For me, there was "Abe" and "F.C." Abe was a construction worker who could live on less food than any other prisoner in the Camp. He gave me a great deal of food which he could have sold for cigarettes. Not Abe. I will always be indebted to him for his attitude toward his food. After the war, Abe had a construction company which was headquartered about 30 miles west of where my wife and I lived. I told Abe I would help him with his books of the business for free until he was well on his way. He did, and then continued to use more and more of my time, so I had to shut him down. I still had to support my family and thus earn a living. I couldn't seem to make Abe understand. Such is one of life's disappointments. I did so hate to disappoint Abe.

F.C. was another construction worker from Wake and of course, a civilian. I had substituted for F.C. on his Capital News paper route when we were kids. We grew up about three blocks from each other. He came from a wonderful family: a sister and two brothers. F.C. wanted to be a doctor and did become a dermatologist after the war. F.C. died of a heart attack, in 1989, while trying to climb out of the Grand Canyon in Arizona.

Life in the Niigata camp was about the same as in Kawasaki, except the guards weren't quite as vicious. We walked about six miles to work on the docks every day. We had a lot of Bataan Death March POWs with us in Niigata, in addition to many Canadians.

Four men were assigned to a work crew, which would load a 44,000-pound freight railroad coal car, with yeh-ho baskets (two) slung from a pole over the shoulder, all during one work day. Two of the men loaded the baskets on the ground and the other two with their full baskets, would walk up a plank to the top of the car, walk down the length of the car on a plank, dump the baskets and walk down another plank to the filling station to reload with the coal.

Each basket weighed about 75 pounds, which meant a 110-pound man was carrying 150 pounds of coal. Of course, we would all get a turn shoveling. You had to make a trip up the planks about every five minutes to finish the car in a work day or else you didn't eat that night. We didn't know it then, but POWs were at the other end of the coal production cycle, mining this very coal.

Our guards were military instead of the usual civilian cops, which I suppose made a difference in the treatment. One day the guards took us all down to the estuary and let us go for a swim. Man alive,

177

but the swim was wonderful. While we were swimming, a ship blew up right in front of us, from a proximity floating mine which had been dropped by a U.S. Air Force B-29.

We were in the Niigata camp for four months until August 1945.

THE SOLACE OF PRAYER

God sends his angels to help in prayer

To those of heartache everywhere.

God knows no end of instant grace

For strays and sinners in this worldly place.

So I carried the coal, day without end

Knowing that my God someday would send

The forces needed to quell the din

Thank God I'd found my World Within.

— dkk

Recognizing Niigata was never damaged whatsoever by bombings, we were curious as to why the United States was keeping the city unscathed by the lethal elements from the B-29s. We didn't know then, but the powers-that-be in the U.S. were saving certain cities for a little test program which it had going.

In May 1945, the B-29s' night over-flights began escalating to where we may have 30 or 40 planes in a time frame from sundown to sunup. At first, we could not imagine what they were doing for we could never hear any explosion, which we should hear even though we were miles from the center of town. Then one day we understood. On the way to work, we saw a large floating proximity mine laying along the side of the road. The planes were laying mines in the estuary by the hundreds.

The B-29s would shut down their engines far out over the Sea of Japan, coast in over Niigata, lay their aerial proximity mines, rev up their engines and climb out for the return trip to China, from whence they came.

In July 1945, while we were working in the docks loading coal or whatever, we would watch one ship after another settle on the bottom of the estuary as their bowels were blown out by these mines. If a ship came within a certain distance of one of the mines, the mine was drawn to the ship by magnetism.

After a month or so, the harbor was literally pockmarked with ships partially-sunken but visible when resting on the bottom of the shallow estuary.

The entrance to the harbor, by August, was practically closed to shipping.

Along about this time, a work party of Americans and Canadians were unloading a small ship of five-gallon cans of alcohol plus another unknown element. The prisoners could make out the Nip characters for alcohol but were unable to identify the characters for the unknown element.

They all wanted to drink some of the joy-juice but were wary of the unknown substance. Some Americans talked the Canadians into trying the yellowish liquid, supposedly made from pineapples. They really were high after a few swigs of the joy-juice. Then all at once, they started to keel over like tenpins.

Eight of them died immediately. The other element was formaldehyde and was placed in the alcohol to keep the Nip populace from drinking it. The liquid was to be used for anti-freeze for autos and trucks.

During the latter part of July 1945, we could see the Nips had picked one of the sunken cargo ships to store barges of ordnance and ammunition on, thinking no one would attack a sunken ship which was listing to one side.

One day about noon, we could hear the sweet sound of a multitude of American engines humming directly above us in the clouds. All at once, we could hear them starting to scream. Then out of the clouds they came, one after another and all of them going for pre-assigned targets. Or so it appeared.

Three or four of the U.S. Navy planes headed straight for the sunken ammo ship and from that moment on, for several days, the ship was exploding. We would finish a day's work, go back to the camp and, sure enough, the next day when we got to work, we would watch some more fireworks. With the appearance of the

Navy fighters, we knew the end was in sight. However, we worried about the end, for the Nips continually told us that if the American troops landed on Honshu, they would kill all of us, as they did the men we had left on Wake.

They, about 100 men, were lined up on the edge of a trench they had dug, and were slaughtered, landing in a common grave.

THE COMMON GRAVE

Each man that day who dug the grave

Did he pray to God his soul to save?

What were his thoughts when his time had come,

For each man that fell was some woman's son.

What caused the enemy to take their lives?

Was it vengeance, hate or other strife?

Until we join our Lord above

Our enemy we must learn to love.

— dkk

FREEDOM'S CURSE

Youths scream for freedom but soon they'll find

Its Babylon sin and Jezebel wine.

Their newly-found freedom will lend them no voice

In ending, it hands them chains of their choice.

Freedom's not meant for casting your lines

And retrieving while snagging whatever one finds.

Freedom means caring for God's world herein

His solace you'll find through God's discipline.

So if you want to be free, present it to Christ

But never complain when he hands you the price.

And carefully be with your choice of prayers

For you may be surprised with the answer He shares.

— dkk

CHAPTER 16

The Earthly Resurrection

About the 15th of August, we hit the dirt floor of the barracks, ran out to the benjo, sounded off, and ate our cup of barley. Then the call came to "Fall Out"… THEN THE UNEXPECTED HAPPENED!!!!!!!

We lined up to march the seven or eight miles to work. We stood in ranks for about 30 minutes, wondering what was happening. Then the Nip interpreter came out and told us to go back to the barracks.

Then it dawned on us. The Allies had landed on Honshu. This meant the Nipponese were going to keep their promise to slaughter us all in the event of the expected landing. We would be taken out into the fields to dig our mass grave. Then they would line us up on the edge of our grave and from the machine guns guarding us, open fire. Oh, God, not after all we have been through during the last four years, don't let this happen!

The only days we didn't work were the Emperor's birthday and our Christmas. You have never seen a bunch of men so nervous. And talk about scuttlebutt, it rolled out of the human mouths like oral diarrhea.

Finally, all the guards were summoned to the camp commander's area for a briefing. Our most proficient interpreter was a French-Canadian. And could the man speak Japanese? Wow! Later, he assembled the prisoners, all 1000 of us. He told us we probably would not believe the message which he was about to explain to us.

He said the Emperor of Japan had accepted an unconditional surrender of the armed forces of Japan to the Allies, and in two days, Allied planes would be coming in with food and clothing for us.

We were told to build a huge "PW" sign on the hill above the prison compound, about 100 feet tall, to enable the planes to find us. The Nips were also told by General MacArthur prisoners were not to be molested by Nip troops or civilians or there would be "hell to pay." The Nips had a great deal of respect for MacArthur and took him at his word. The interpreter also told us we would be leaving the island of Honshu as soon as the arrangements could be made.

No one should be subject to transposition of one's mental composure with such suddenness. I can specifically remember that I became suddenly ill. I ran to the benjo and puked. I had spent all of these days, months and years preparing for my certain death. I had banished any thought of happiness, home, loved ones, comfort, memories and freedom from my consciousness; living only in a grey, drab void looking for my Savior in Heaven.

And now the world would expect me to do a complete 180 degree turn around and conform to their standards (if you can call the mores and social system by which we live "standards"). I would be

THE EARTHLY RESURRECTION

24 years old this coming October 7, 1945, and felt like I had lived at least 100 years.

I was sick for several days, not knowing why. And now a terrible fear suddenly gripped my inner being.

What if this was a horrible trick by the Nips, or

What if all this was a dream and soon I would awaken to the daily bugle call, or

What if I were to be killed by the civilian population (crazed by the humiliation of defeat after all they had sacrificed), or

What if my loved ones had died without my telling them how much I loved them, or

What if I were killed during the transport to my beloved country, or

What if this "carrot" was to be hung before my eyes, only to lead me to a life which was worse than the experience of the last four years?

I know this will sound a bit "looney," but I knew at times in the future, I was going to miss my little game I had played in the POW days when every thought was sifted through the grey bottomless pit known to me as my soul, and nothing, I mean nothing in life had any value whatsoever. And at times, before leaving the camp, I found myself resenting the outside world, represented by the Allied Forces, for intruding upon my "World Within" and often thought, "How dare they intrude upon the secure peace of mind I had created through my acceptance of the absolutus?"

The day after the big, and I mean big, news was given to us about the Nip surrender, there was a large U.S. Naval Task Force lying off the east coast of Honshu. The task force commanded by Halsey was only a few hundred miles east of our camp in Niigata. This was the task force which had previously attacked, with fighters and bombers, the docks where we worked only a few days earlier.

Around noon, we were in the compound patiently waiting for something to happen when suddenly, we heard the now-pleasant drone of American airplane engines and then came manna from heaven. The time of year was August and in the summer we only wore a "g-string," which barely hid our genitals. The Nips always made sure we had something to wear so their females would not see our genitals.

As the planes neared the camp, we could see they were flying fairly low. There were probably 20 TBMs and a few Grumman fighters in the bunch. They made a low-level group pass over us and then swung around and one by one, let their wheels down and opened the bomb-bay to fly as slow as possible over us. We could see the guys in the bomb-bays taking pictures of us. As they would pass over, they would throw out the partially empty packs of cigarettes they had in their pockets. Because we appeared nude to the airman, some of them managed to take off their coats, shirts, shoes, pants and socks to drop down to us on the next pass. Can't you just see the flight officer's face when those planes landed on the aircraft carrier's flight deck and the air crews stepped out of the plane onto the deck half-naked with only their skivvies on?

THE EARTHLY RESURRECTION

You talk about an exhilarating moment in your life, you are standing practically naked and your mental thermometer is zero, when a huge dive-bomber comes waggling in at 100 feet altitude and 100 miles per hour just to take pictures or say "Hi" to you.

The next day the same planes came back, and as they cruised in over our heads, they dropped sea bags full of everything imaginable. You could tell the men aboard ship had tried to imagine what they would have liked provided for them had they gone through our experience. They had scrounged through the ship and tried to send items such as cigarettes, candy bars, underwear, pants, shoes and petite editions of *Time* magazine.

From the *Time* magazine we learned of the atomic bombs, although we didn't actually realize their deadly impact on human life. We also learned our present location was to be the next in line for one of the "pickles," so to speak.

One of my friends had a bad case of dysentery and was in the benjo. A plane flew over and missed the drop zone in the middle of the compound with a sea bag. And you guessed it, the bag made a direct hit on the "john" and went through to drive my friend right down into the "honey bucket" below. It almost killed the character, and he never was the same again. He never did recognize me again after the incident of the "sea-bag bomb." I heard he died right after reaching the United States shores.

On the fourth or fifth day after "resurrection," B-29 airplanes began coming into our area with POW supplies of food, clothing and medicines. They had their bomb-bay doors open and you could see the pallets upon which the goods were strapped. The pallets were rigged to huge parachutes which would float the supplies down to the drop area, so designated by markings in a huge field. They dropped everything to satisfy our needs. Even fresh milk came down in gas tank containers.

The first pallet I reached was laden with split pea soup. I sat down, opened several cans with a rock and gorged myself. This was a mistake. I became violently ill and started spewing at both ends of the bodily food conduit, both intake and exit.

I was so extremely proud of a new pair of GI shoes and khaki pants and shirt. I even had a pair of new socks to wear though my feet were covered with open sores. And soap, oh, the lovely soap with which to bathe. How wonderful it was. I carried the bar of soap around in my pocket for some weeks after, just in case the war broke out of the confines of human endeavor. I also took some clothes and hid them in case of an emergency.

At the time, my head was swollen to almost twice its size by a huge cyst. The cyst broke in a few days and poured out the poison like an oil-gusher, then my head return to normal before we started traveling.

THE ROAD BACK

The endless road back

To the values I once knew,

Will weave and meander

Through tribulation anew.

I can never return

To the bygone plateau,

Time will not heal

One's own damaged soul.

I'll live out this life

In my "World Within,"

Our world is with God

But not without sin.

— dkk

The "now" world would require I start the long, formidable journey on the road back to what "they" call the precepts of Western civilization. I would be required to . . .

    . . . apply the wrong emphasis to a value . . .

    . . . acquiesce with 'their' thin moral fiber . . .

    . . . be polite to people whom I do not respect . . .

    . . . feel disgust for capitalistic ethics . . .

    . . . listen to politicians expound on rhetorical garbage . . .

    . . . watch while our country spirals toward Babylon . . .

    . . . speak of dangers and no one to listen . . . .

And the list goes on and on and on and on.

A few days after the startling news of the Nip surrender, a fellow I will call A.K. (marine) and I thought we would go nuts sitting in the compound waiting for the arrival of "something or somebody" from the Allies, so we decided to take a walk. We probably shouldn't have left the security of the compound for the Nip guards had all melted into the populace and a few civilian police took their place as our "protectors." A.K. and I hiked a couple of miles to the northeast of the compound, up toward the mountains. We came to a small village, and the populace came out to greet us. We knew a few words of their language and managed to communicate the news about the end of the war. They had already heard about the surrender on their radios.

There was one elderly man who invited us to lunch with his family. We went to his small, straw and paper house with a thatch roof, took off our shoes and entered. The man had a wife and two daughters. The man, A.K., and I sat down on our haunches before a small table while the wife and daughters sat at another table in the background. I remember thinking the daughters were extremely pretty. Of course, after I was able to start adding weight on to the fat-free 105 pounds which I weighed on the big-news-day, I started noticing the opposite sex.

The Nip told us he had three sons in the war and he knew one had been killed, he knew not where. In fact he didn't know where his other two were, but presumed they were alive. His wife soon started cooking some food for us. A stew of fish and some veggies accompanied by the ever-present rice. Also, they served us some saki which was delicious. What astounded me was the complete absence of animosity in their attitude toward us. It seemed they were more or less relieved to see the end of the hostilities.

I expected my shoes to be missing when I stepped outside on the threshold but the Nip assured me you could leave the shoes there to the end of time and no one would touch them. Stealing was a serious criminal offense in Japan. We thanked the family profusely and returned to the compound.

CHAPTER 17

The Exodus

On about the fifth day subsequent to the "Big Revelation" of free-dom, a man parachuted into the compound from a dive-bomber. It was an ex-governor of Michigan, Harold Stassen, who was on the staff of Admiral Halsey of the Task Force previously referenced. He told us many things about which we were curious. He mentioned the blond women of the U.S. were as beautiful as when we left the States some five years earlier. He told us about the A-bombs and the surrender.

Also, he mentioned that not all of the prisoners could fly back to the States but some would take the ships home. MacArthur had halted all transportation and communication utilities but was al-lowing a train to move in the system to meet us in about two or three days at the downtown terminal. This train would take us to the city of Tokyo where we would be trans-shipped to Yokohama and the docks or airbase. Stassen then walked down to an airstrip nearby and mounted a plane which took him back to the carrier from whence he came.

When it came time to leave for the train depot, we were missing a considerable number of men. We knew where they had gone; as soon as a man gets his belly full of good food, he starts the age-old custom of chasing women. Later on, the occupation troops found a number of the missing in the cathouses of Niigata. I guess I was not inclined to chase as yet, being in the throes of health recovery.

We were told never to try retribution on the former Nip guards or Jap army personnel or we would be shot by our MPs. For some reason, I never seemed to hold much animosity toward the enemy after hostilities had ended. During the war, I could gladly have shot each one, of many, between the eyes from a distance of two feet, while looking them squarely in their eyes.

The day to embark on the train finally came. We walked the four or five miles to the depot and mounted the passenger cars. A number of Nip army guards were on the train for protection from the populace and, to my knowledge, there were no incidents of violence.

We rode for about 24 hours and finally arrived in Tokyo. We were allowed to disembark but had to stay in ranks on the station platform. There were several hundred MPs surrounding the total train station to make sure none of us broke out to harass the populace.

A colonel of the MPs came over to me and asked if my name was "Dare Kibble." I answered affirmative and he said a soldier wanted to see me further down the dock platform. I followed him to where a nice looking uniformed girl was standing. I looked at her so intensely, she probably thought I intended to rape her. But who in the world would be looking for me halfway around the world. She said, "You don't know me, my name is Marie Cook. I am a cousin to a man named Willie Cook who married your sister, Mary. And I told them I would watch for you in Tokyo." You talk about heavenly and celestial guidance. Wow! We talked for a few minutes with the MP colonel standing by and then the colonel said I had to go. He "escorted" me back to the ranks and we boarded another train for Yokohama.

Upon arrival in Yokohama, we disembarked and were again warned not to try any funny stuff. There were MPs everywhere by the thousands.

We were escorted to a compound and told to park all belongings, including any memorabilia, until we were stripped naked. We were told we would be able to return and gather any of our belongings later. We went through a shed where we were deloused and segregated as to "by ship or by plane." We were never allowed to return to our belongings. Those people running the delousing operation took all of our memorabilia for themselves to impress the people at home, naturally at the expense of the men who really earned the honors, if any. Just another manifestation of the "World Without."

Along about this time, I realized my life was entering a new plateau, and I envisioned the "World Within." I knew I must co-exist with the "Outside World's" morals and ethics if I were to perform some of the functions I needed so dearly to fulfill my soul-searching, such as marriage, children, home life, the love of dear ones. Yet my inner being screamed at me to never, never relinquish the salve-of-the-soul experience of knowing the Lord during the pits of hell in the prison camps of the Orient. During my years as a prisoner, my "World Without" was my "World Within," one and the same. But now I knew they would separate and present me with innumerable decisions, some right and some sinful.

Into this atmosphere of conflict I reluctantly entered at the end of World War II in August 1945.

I was put aboard the ship USS *Ozark* for my trip home. It was a ship built to carry mechanized armor vehicles. It was a new ship and had every convenience to cater to warriors going into battle or coming out of battle.

We were allowed to take as many showers as our raw skins could stand. If a person goes without bathing for an extended period of time, the skin tends to scale somewhat like a fish. Upon bathing, all of the scales fall and your skin becomes raw and bleeds at times. They didn't have too much extra food for they didn't expect 1000 of us on board.

We sailed out of Tokyo Bay on the 2nd of September, 1945, going past the *Missouri* while the surrender was officially being signed on her decks.

We were to go to Guam before going on to Hawaii en route home. When we disembarked at Guam, we were taken to a large field hospital. They really didn't know what to do for our emaciated bodies. They shot us full of penicillin and spread sulfa on our sores.

We walked around the hospital grounds for exercise and came upon a Red Cross tent, where, as I mentioned earlier, we learned the difference between the Red Cross and the Salvation Army. We had no money and everything we wanted except food sold for money. The Red Cross said they would loan us $10 provided we would sign a promissory note to be paid later. Can you believe the SOBs, after all we sacrificed for their liberty and country? We all told them to "shove it where the sun don't shine" and went on down to the Salvation Army tent.

The Salvation Army gave us each ten dollars, coffee, doughnuts, and a pack of cigs for nothing. I probably needn't add whereas in the last 45 years I have never given a dime to the Red Cross knowingly. In fact, I almost was fired on one job, later in life, because I wouldn't contribute to the United Way of which the Red Cross bled some of their money.

The first night when we were in Guam, the mess hall told us, we could have anything our hearts desired except women. There were 1004 of us and believe it or not, we consumed 8000 loaves of bread and 1000 pounds of butter. In addition, some of the guys ate steaks.

By the time dinner was over, most of the ten dollars per man received from the Salvation Army, through a crap game had funneled down into a few hands. We had a beautiful blond head nurse in our ward. The guy next to me had won considerable money and called the blond beauty, all the time complaining of pain. When the nurse arrived at his sack, the character asked the nurse, "Would you like to earn a couple hundred bucks?" She said, "No thank you." The character was persistent and said, "How about five hundred bucks?" The blond said, "You know I could have you thrown in the brig for propositioning me." The guy said, "Listen lady, I could take all of your brig time you could hand me, laughing every minute." He said, "Where do you think I've been for the last four years?" Later on that night, the blond beauty even laughed with us about the proposition. She didn't know where we had been, it turned out.

After a couple of days, the upper crust loaded us back on *Ozark* and we headed for Hawaii. The trip was beautiful and we ran a race with a carrier which had another load of POWs. We won the race and several days later we entered Pearl Harbor.

No one met us except some intelligence officers. All hands had to stay on the ship. The civilian authorities were terrified as to what we would do to their females, cocktail lounges, and other places of excitement.

The intelligence guys picked four men to question at their head-quarters. The men they picked were a marine, a sailor, a civilian and a dogface. I happened to be the sailor. A captain in the Navy was in charge of the interrogation. His name was "Foss," a name I was to become familiar with in my days in the Puget Sound area in the state of Washington. Also, we had a tug boat at Wake which had belonged to his company. The Intel wanted to know where we had been during the imprisonment, the type of treatment received, the food received, when we were moved and the Allied action which we had observed.

After the interrogation, Captain Foss said there was a car and a driver available to us for going anywhere on the island. He knew we couldn't do much harm to the populace with no money in our khaki pockets. By voice vote, we all wanted to go to one place, a grocery store.

The driver took us to the largest grocery store on the island. When we entered, we must have looked like a freakish outfit. We oooohed and aaaaahed for about two hours at all the wonderful chow available and didn't buy a thing. We absolutely could not believe all of this food was available to a society which knew positively nothing about appreciating one's livelihood.

The next day we were back on the *Ozark*, headed for the Golden Gate. In POW camp we had an idiom of, "The Golden Gate in 48." We talked among ourselves about the possibility of a renegade Nip sub still on the hunt and possibly sinking our ship. Such a turn of events would be the final irony.

In about four days, one morning I looked up into the grey overcast skies and there was one of the most beautiful man-made structures I would ever see, the Golden Gate Bridge.

No one knows the tremendous oppressive weighting which dissipated from my body at the wonderful sight. It is beyond the capability of any language expression. I thought I must explode from the sheer ecstasy.

I had made it home!

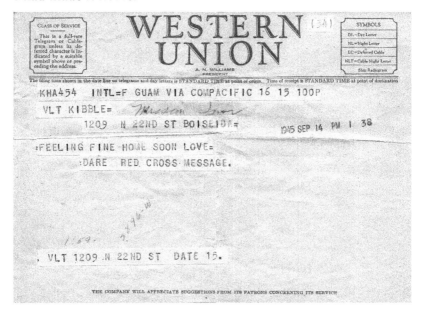

Western Union telegram from Dare to his parents, September 14, 1945.

EPILOGUE

By Maggie Kibble Newhouse

The minute the released POWs got on the boat from Japan, they were made to line up on the ship, holding on to two steel bars, and were hosed down with firehoses to delouse them. Dad said that hurt like hell—and afterward his skin was raw. When they got back to the States, they spent two months rehydrating and nourishing the men in a debriefing camp before they were allowed to go home. After he returned to Boise, my dad had to report to a Navy hospital in Corvallis once a month, to check in, to make sure he was alright.

When my dad came home to Boise in October from the debriefing camp, he met my mom the night he arrived. My parents were married six weeks after they met, in December. They met because my mom and his sister were best friends. Both women served as telephone operators during the war, working the night shifts. All wartime communication came by telephone at that time, and they were privy to a lot of high-level information. My mom, Anne Smith Sund, was married once before, but her husband, Gil Sund, was killed in WW II. He was an Army Air Corps navigator and was killed soon after they married.

Dare Keane Kibble (center) with his father, Monk (Marion Kibble), and Dare's dog Teddy. Photo taken at the Boise Train Depot on October 14, 1945.

My dad came from an alcoholic family, and he drank a lot; I don't know if it was the family thing or PTSD. He was a functioning alcoholic—he worked full time and also went to school at the University of Idaho full time. He was brilliant. And then my parents started having kids. If he was covering up something, or running from something, I don't know what it was. He always had a job—and was good at what he did, and if he lost it, he went on to something better.

He got his bachelor's degree and his master's degree, right after WW II, and studied for and obtained his CPA, and went to work as an accountant. I was very proud of him for doing that, for getting an education. Before he went into the war, he would have been voted least likely to succeed. He also ran a tax practice on the side. He was very precise and perfectionistic in his work, so to find something wrong, or being done incorrectly, was upsetting to him. He always called a spade a spade, and sometimes it cost him his job. He was also very crusty, a salt of the earth kind of guy. He could be pretty tough, but he was actually a pussy cat. He was a tough and tender kind of guy. If he didn't like something, he would say it. If it wasn't right, he would say it. He liked a good challenge, and he liked a good argument. He retired from the IRS as an excise tax auditor and expert tax witness. He traveled a lot with that job, and was often gone two months at a time.

He loved his family fiercely, loved his outdoors, and his freedom. He was very patriotic, but wasn't obnoxious about it. He loved a political debate. He exercised his right to vote, and encouraged people to vote, and emphasized that it is a privilege to be able to vote. He often told people that if you don't take advantage of these opportunities, they go away. He would use his war experience to push the envelope sometimes.

Dad quit drinking when I was fourteen, in 1977. He was 57. And then he quit smoking right after that. That was a horrible time. It was a family death that made my dad quit drinking.

He had many health problems. He had malaria—lifetime malaria. He had night sweats a lot; my mom changed the sheets almost every day. He had ulcers (there was a lot of scar tissue, presumably from all of the filth and malnutrition over the years). He had all his teeth but lots of weird gum diseases, again probably from the malnutrition he endured. He had a major heart attack at 78 and survived it, needing six bypasses. At the time, the doctor informed us that he had had several previous minor heart attacks, which we didn't realize. He used to have blackouts, which we thought were migraines, but maybe they were heart attacks.

I think that writing his memoir was therapeutic for him. He became a far more compassionate man after it was completed. His spiritual life also grew. Near the end of his life, he regularly wrote letters to the editor of the Idaho Statesman newspaper and gained a reputation for that.

He fought the U.S. government for twenty years, and finally in the last ten to twelve years of his life, he was granted a 100% disability. One remarkable thing about my dad's story is, how many people do you know who were in a Japanese POW camp for four years, who lived in the state of Idaho? And unlike those who were civilians on Wake Island and got paid for their time in POW camps, he never got the five years of back pay for his time as a POW, because his records were destroyed at Pearl Harbor.

Abbey's Poem

Grandfather: Hero

You are my everlasting
Hero.

You are fearless and
Funny, a quite colorful
Character.

Fighting for your freedom
And the freedom of the
Future so that I might grow
Up in a better nation, and a
Better time.
You preserved my future.
I sing praise to your
Name, you are my hero!

As I picture your great
Body and your longing soul
In a prison of hate and
Death I weep in thanks
And pride.
I can say proudly that my

Grandfather was a true
Patriot to his country!

You have brought pride and
Great expectations to this
Family.
You are my everlasting hero.

Telling many tales of
Comedy of those years
Of hate and death,
Each enthusiastically
Funny, but each holding a
Fear, a fact, and doubtless
Courage.

I hold you in my heart
Forever with the deepest
Respect, forever in my hero
And forever my friend!

—Abbey Stickley
DKK's Granddaughter

ACKNOWLEDGMENTS

I'd like to thank Fred, my husband, for the support in getting this project finally to print. I thank my kids, Abbey, David, Max, and Will for their love for their grandfather, and also my siblings Howard (deceased), Alan (Linda), and Linda (Ron), and the rest of Dare's grandchildren, and the many nieces and nephews that my father loved so dearly. And to my mother Anne, whom my father loved deeply.

Thanks to the team at Aloha Publishing, including Maryanna Young, Hannah Cross, and Jennifer Regner, and the Fusion Creative Works team, Shiloh Schroeder, Rachel Langaker, and Jessie Carpenter.

ABOUT THE AUTHOR

Dare Keane Kibble was a Navy war hero and World War II POW. He was a POW from December 1941 to August 1945. Dare married Anne Smith Sund, whom he met the first day he returned to Boise from POW camp. He went on with his life, earning a bachelor's and a master's degree in accounting from the University of Idaho, and went to work as a CPA, tax auditor, computer programmer and expert tax witness. He loved his family fiercely, loved his outdoors, and his freedom. He believed in the constitution, and why we need the military. He encouraged his sons to join the military, and they did—and so did his grandchildren. He was intensely patriotic. He was known for absolute honesty, and for "calling a spade a spade." His daughter, Maggie Kibble Newhouse, is the youngest of four children and is responsible for bringing the exact manuscript her father wrote to life.

Maggie Kibble Newhouse is the daughter of Dare Keane Kibble. Maggie was born and raised in Boise, Idaho. She learned her love of country from her parents, who were also both Treasure Valley natives. Maggie is a wife, a grandmother, the mother of four, and a business woman. She really does believe her father was a hero, and a lot of people don't have heroes as parents. She feels privileged to be able to put this book together so others will know her father's story, and understand what he and others who served in WW II did for their country.

NOTES

1.   "Gyrene" is a slang term marines have used for themselves since the 1920s. See www.ww2gyrene.org.

2.   F.D. Gross, *Wake Island Wig-Wag*, a newsletter produced by the Defenders of Wake Island (an organization), Independence, Mo. 64052.

3.   Winfield Scott Cunningham, *Wake Island Command*, Little, Brown and Company (Boston, MA, 1961).

4.   Ibid. Quotes taken from pages 24-25, 129-132, 267-268.

5.   Oswald Chambers, *My Utmost For His Highest*, Dodd, Mead & Company (New York, NY, 1935).

6.   Definition of "civilize," *Merriam-Webster Dictionary*.

7.   Oswald Chambers, *My Utmost For His Highest*, Dodd, Mead & Company (New York, NY, 1935).

CPSIA information can be obtained
at www.ICGtesting.com
Printed in the USA
FSHW010611060721
82983FS